PUBLIC TELEVISION

Recent Titles in
Contributions to the Study of Mass Media and Communications

PUBLIC
TELEVISION

Panacea, Pork Barrel,
or Public Trust?

Marilyn Lashley

Contributions to the Study of Mass Media
and Communications, Number 33

GREENWOOD PRESS
New York • Westport, Connecticut • London

Library of Congress Cataloging-in-Publication Data

Lashley, Marilyn, 1946–
   Public television : panacea, pork barrel, or public trust? /
Marilyn Lashley.
     p. cm.—(Contributions to the study of mass media and
communications, ISSN 0732–4456 ; no. 33)
   Includes bibliographical references and index.
   ISBN 0–313–27964–0 (alk. paper)
   1. Public television—United States. I. Title. II. Series.
HE8700.79.U6L37   1992
384.55′06′573—dc20   91–34482

British Library Cataloguing in Publication Data is available.

Library of Congress Catalog Card Number: 91–34482
ISBN: 0–313–27964–0
ISSN: 0732–4456

First published in 1992

Greenwood Press, 88 Post Road West, Westport, CT 06881
An imprint of Greenwood Publishing Group, Inc.

Printed in the United States of America

The paper used in this book complies with the
Permanent Paper Standard issued by the National
Information Standards Organization (Z39.48–1984).

10 9 8 7 6 5 4 3 2 1

To Lebasi, Yorel, and Pearline

Contents

Tables and Figures

Tables

Figures

Abbreviations

ACNO	Advisory Council of National Organizations
APB	Association for Public Broadcasting
CPB	Corporation for Public Broadcasting
CSG	Community Service Grant
CTW	Children's Television Workshop
EOP	Executive Office of the President
FCC	Federal Communications Commission
HEW	Health, Education and Welfare
NAB	National Association of Broadcasters
NAEB	National Association of Educational Broadcasters
NAPTS	National Association of Public Television Stations
NBMC	National Black Media Coalition
NEH	National Endowment for the Humanities
NET	National Educational Television
NPR	National Public Radio
NTIA	National Telecommunications and Information Administration
OE	Office of Education
OMB	Office of Management and Budget

OTP   Office of Telecommunications Policy

PBS   Public Broadcasting Service

PTFP   Public Telecommunications Facilities Program

PTV   Public Television

SECA   Southern Educational Communications Association

SPC   Station Program Cooperative

TCAF   Temporary Commission on Alternative Financing for
              Public Telecommunications

Acknowledgments

This book is the fruit of many labors. The author is indebted to Paul Hirsch, Norman Bradburn, Pastora San Juan Cafferty, Russell Hardin, Edward Laumann, and John Padgett for their encouragement and invaluable expertise over the course of the project. The author also appreciates the assistance and comments on the manuscript given by staff of the Brookings Institution and its Governmental Studies Division, especially former Director Paul Peterson and Director Thomas Mann, Kent Weaver, John Chubb, and Joseph White. In addition, the author earnestly thanks management and staff of the Corporation for Public Broadcasting, the Public Broadcasting Service, the Association for Public Broadcasting (formerly, NAPTS), and public television stations, in particular, Thomas Fuller, Rick Grefe, Pat King, Young Lee, Mildred Morse, Helene Weisz, Joseph Widoff, John Fuller, Dale Rhodes, Peter Fannon, Kelly Siegel, and William McCarter. A special note of thanks goes to the public television stations, congressional staff, OMB examiners, and CPB and PBS staff who responded to the many rounds of surveys and interviews. Moreover, the author is grateful to Norelisha Crawford, Kevin Hart, and Cynthia Dawkins, who provided indispensable assistance with the preparation of this manuscript.

The author is also indebted to the Brookings Institution, the National Science Foundation (grant SES-842008), and the University of Maryland at College Park for research support on particular stages of this project.

Although this book would not exist without the assistance of those named—and others not identified herein—the author is responsible for all errors of fact.

Introduction

Panacea, pork barrel, or public trust? The debate over public broadcasting policy and public television performance continues. Twenty-five years after its inception, the Corporation for Public Broadcasting is still struggling with an identity problem and floundering as a public organization. Critics question whether public television has changed from a panacea for a public interested in the medium's educational uses to a pork barrel for public television industry professionals, and whether it is even capable of becoming the "public" trust its initiators envisioned. Deemed by some observers as "a poverty program for the well to do," by others as a "country club and old boy network for industry professionals," and by still others as "overly cautious," "a name without a concept," and "paradise postponed," all agree that public television has consistently failed to cope with some serious organizational problems.

POLICY IMPLICATIONS

Citing Congress's failure to provide long-range federal funding, ongoing political interference, and failure to take programming risks, formerly ardent advocates assert that public television has not lived up to its potential, despite significant budgetary growth. Is public broadcasting policy so broadly defined that it most effectively serves only a highbrow audience and narrow interests within the industry? Or does the Corporation for Public Broadcasting support and promote noncommercial broadcasting that best serves the public interest, convenience, and necessity? To these and attendant questions, opinion is divided. However, advocates and critics concur that public broadcasting fails to live up to its promise as a government-financed organization.

In order to evaluate effectiveness in the public organization and explain public television performance over time, the focus of this book is the Corporation for Public Broadcasting, the instrument of public broadcasting policy.[1] This book is a chronicle of the birth and expansion of public television; in it, we tell how and why public television is repeatedly transformed. In this book, we will discern how a public organization can experience as much budgetary growth as public broadcasting and still be the object of such salient criticism on its record of organizational performance. We will ascertain why the goals of public television are continually redefined as it routinely searches for increased federal funding, even though it is a highly regarded public good. Moreover, we will discuss what this quest forebodes for the more typical public policy, whose goals and strategies are even more ill-defined, contentious, or publicly fractious.

When one examines the history of public television in the United States, one wonders whether public television can realize its public policy mission. From its origins as an idea shared by a coalition of special interest groups, public television has evolved into a complex telecommunications system comprised by hundreds of autonomous entities licensed by the Federal Communications Commission and supported by the Corporation for Public Broadcasting. In its efforts to serve many varied interests over the years, public television seems to have shifted from serving the broad interests of a diverse public to serving the more narrow interests of viewer checkwriters and industry professionals. Is public television a pork barrel for public television professionals? Is public television even capable of providing a truly "public" service?

What the story of public television shows us is that public policy can fall far short or even fail to meet the expectations of decision makers and special interests (coalition partners), although it successfully secures increased federal funding by adjusting to the everchanging task demands of its external environment. Whether and how the Corporation for Public Broadcasting copes with the complexities and uncertainties of its external environment is not only instructive for this particular public organization, it is also instructive for public policy in general.

Generally, the evaluation of effectiveness in any organization is fraught with analytical problems. However, in this book, a method of assessment is used that examines the public organization's unique attributes, the legislative mandate and federal funding. Particular attention is given to these attributes, and organization theory is used to explain behavior and evaluate effectiveness in the Corporation of Public Broadcasting with respect to public television.

Herein, the public organization is viewed as the instrument of public policy. Herein, the public organization's dependence upon political actors for its creation and maintenance—survival—is perceived as essential to the assessment of organizational effectiveness. Herein, special attention is given to the public organization's decision-making (appropriations) process, issues and outcomes. To this end, the following questions are addressed: What is public broadcasting? What is public television? How are they organized? What are the goals of public television? Is it effective? Why or why not? Who benefits from public television? Whose interests are served?

THE CASE OF PUBLIC BROADCASTING

The Corporation for Public Broadcasting is a public organization, a legislatively mandated and government-financed organization that provides a public service and performs an administrative function[2]. Although some public broadcasters disclaim this classification, the Corporation for Public Broadcasting provides a public service, performs an administrative function, is subject to congressional and executive oversight, and receives regular appropriations like other government bureaucracies. Therefore, throughout this book, it is evaluated as a public organization.

Public broadcasting was conceived as a national network of educational television stations. Public broadcasting policy was formulated to meet an array of goals from various special interest groups concerned about the development and use of the potentially powerful, new medium—television. Manufacturers of telecommunications equipment, broadcasters, concerned citizens, church and community groups, educators, and philanthropies concertedly lobbied for federal involvement and protection of noncommercial broadcasting. The outcome was the establishment of a government-financed organization to develop and support noncommercial television and radio as a public service.

Legally, the Corporation for Public Broadcasting is a private nonprofit corporation authorized by Congress and financed through the appropriations process. Mandated in 1967, the Corporation for Public Broadcasting distributes federal funding and provides supportive assistance to noncommercial telecommunications entities throughout the United States. Public television is the determinant and more costly nationwide public telecommunications system supported by the Corporation for Public Broadcasting, which also supports a nationwide system of public radio.[3]

Politically, the Corporation is highly vulnerable to partisan influence. Dependent upon the appropriations process for financing, public broadcasting frequently is subject to changes in congressional and presidential performance preferences that determine its budgetary fortunes. Economically, public broadcasting competes with other public organizations in an environment characterized by budgetary scarcity and uncertainty.

Organizationally, public broadcasting is a veritable hodgepodge of public telecommunications entities and activities. The Corporation for Public Broadcasting and the loose federation of public telecommunications entities it supports share an organizational form and mission little understood by the very public it is authorized to serve. Some viewers can neither distinguish the roles of the Corporation for Public Broadcasting (CPB) and the Public Broadcasting Service (PBS), which serves public television, from those of the local stations nor describe the relationship between them. Others think PBS provides services to both public television and public radio.

In fact, the Corporation for Public Broadcasting is an anomaly among public organizations. It is a public organization that is endowed with broadly based support, yet its mission and organization are not publicly well understood. It is also a public organization protected by special status as a government-sponsored enterprise, yet it is highly vulnerable to political influence. This book explains these dichotomies.

Unlike many public organizations, public broadcasting has nearly complete constituency, congressional, and executive support. Frequently deemed a true "public good" by some legislators, public broadcasting has goals that are not controversial or publicly divisive. Public broadcasting also has a generally well-accepted mission—"to serve the public interest, convenience, [and] necessity."[4] Most important, unlike many public organizations and in spite of its policy appeal, broad public support and the legal latitude and autonomy usually afforded by the special status of government-sponsored enterprise, the Corporation for Public Broadcasting continues to be a target of much discussion, debate, review, and reorganization.

Because it is a federally funded, private, nonprofit corporation enacted by Congress, some policy analysts further distinguish the Corporation for Public Broadcasting as quasi-government or a government-sponsored enterprise. Like all other government-sponsored enterprises, for example, the Tennessee Valley Authority, Fannie Mae, Securities Investor Corporation, and Neighborhood Reinvestment Corporation, public broadcasting enjoys a legal ambiguity that makes it less accountable to government oversight and more autonomous (Seidman, 1988). This special status permits the Corporation to function somewhat outside the established budgetary process—for example, the capability to make budget submissions directly to Congress (bypassing the Office of Management and Budget, OMB) and secure multiyear financing. Within this broad category of government-sponsored enterprises, the Corporation for Public Broadcasting is further differentiated as a private nonprofit organization that is fully owned by the U.S. government, with a Board of Directors appointed by the president.

In practice and despite its status as a government-sponsored enterprise, the Corporation for Public Broadcasting is highly vulnerable to partisan politics. From inception, public broadcasting has languished amidst a sea of budgetary and political uncertainty. Usually, public broadcasting is compelled to cope with this uncertainty by redistributing its budget in keeping with the demands of the more vociferous constituencies, thereby redefining its mission, means, and form in order to survive as a public organization.

THEORETICAL OVERVIEW

Some policy analysts challenge the appropriateness of the application of organization theory to the public organization. Others maintain that the theory provides invaluable insight into understanding performance in public organizations. In this book, adherence is to the latter view. The rational (classical) and resource dependence (environmental) models of organization theory are used to explain performance in the public organization. Two criteria are derived from these models to evaluate public television's record of performance as a public organization: the attainment of legislated goals and survival. The evaluation of organizational effectiveness as the efficient attainment of internally and well-defined goals as specified in the legislative mandate—strategic management—is suggested by the rational model. Alternatively, the evaluation of organizational effectiveness in survival terms, as increased federal appropriations and the retention of coalition partners over time, is suggested by the resource dependence model.

Because the public organization is government-financed and legislatively mandated, it is more dependent upon political markets than economic markets for resources critical to survival. The public organization is dependent upon the mutual adjustment of a coalition of political institutions and actors, namely, the Executive Office of the President, the Office of Management and Budget, Congress and constituents for resource inputs and goals. As decision makers in the public organization toil through the appropriations process, the competing policy preferences of the executive, Congress, constituencies, and specialized interest groups constrain goal attainment. In the public organization, the dependence upon this coalition of actors with disparate goals and the capacity to satisfy their competing expectations, more than rationally derived ends and means, determine what it does and how it does it.

Unlike the private organization in which the consumer is directly linked to the product—and management decides input, throughput, and output—in the public organization, the consumer is detached from the product.[5] Instead, a layer of politicians and bureaucrats both determine means and ends and define what constitutes successful performance. Given this peculiar situation of resource dependence and the instrumentality of coalition formation to goal definition and resource acquisition, the evaluation of public television performance shows that the external environment, rather than internally derived goals with optimal solutions, better explains behavior and decision-making outcomes in the public organization.

Powerful political actors, in their roles as guardians or advocates of public spending, evaluate organizational effectiveness. They assess the public organization's adherence to a legislative mandate, its track record of compliance to their expectations, programmatic justification, and the volume of noise, pro or con, generated by their constituencies. When the public organization is thought to conform to performance expectations and norms of these coalition partners, increased budget appropriations are secured over time. Predictable budgetary growth becomes an end in itself in order to accommodate modest programmatic expansion and inflation. Consequently, stable and predictable budgetary growth over time can serve as an important indicator of effectiveness in public organizations because it reflects successful performance.

Foremost, it is maintained herein that the best explanatory model does not necessarily generate the best prescriptions for behavior in public organizations. Although it is apparent that public organizations may be most adaptive and compliant to the dynamic expectations of the dominant coalition partners in order to secure increased appropriations, it is also demonstrated that the attainment of stated goals becomes subordinate to organizational survival over time. Goals stated in the legislative mandate are frequently diluted as managers of the public organization pursue survival. In this book on public television, the author demonstrates that policies that promote and ensure organizational survival do not, ipso facto, generate the best outcomes for the targets of the policy and can even impede the delivery of service in the public interest.

Two factors are shown to exert substantial influence on effectiveness in public organizations: its situation in a culture characterized by tremendous technical change, resource scarcity, and uncertainty; and its enactment through the efforts of a coalition of special interest groups with shared objectives and disparate means. The examples described in this book demonstrate that the public organization's absolute dependence upon a coalition of special interests and political market forces for resource inputs renders the application of the rational model of organizational behavior less appropriate for the study of public organizations. Consequently, the resource dependence model provides invaluable insight into the behavior of public organizations.

For each model, criteria are imposed that render radically divergent assessments and prescriptions for performance in public organizations. Because public organizations are usually compared with private organizations, most analysts and critics of public television are inclined to evaluate effectiveness in terms of rationally determined goals and optimal solutions. For example, when evaluated by the rational model, perhaps public television can be declared an abject failure given the high degree of organizational fragmentation, political vulnerability, and risk averse—"bland"—programming. Alternatively, when public television is evaluated by the resource dependence model, the assessment is more favorable. Public television can be judged an unqualified success because it generally receives a substantially increased budget appropriation from one year to the next.

METHODOLOGY

The methodology utilized in this book provides an analysis of the role of the external environment on decision making in public organizations. By examining public television policy making from 1967 to 1989, it is demonstrated that decision outcomes are not exclusively dependent upon prior budget decisions. Rather, decision outcomes are dependent upon the public organization's maintenance of stable relationships with decision participants (coalition partners) and its adjustments to contextual changes within its dynamic environment. Contextual changes are defined as external factors that positively or negatively constrain decision making over time.

Presidential, congressional, and constituency support and the economy are shown to exert significant influence over decision making in the public organization. Public television policy is proven to be a function of the interaction of several sets of key decision participants and the organizational pattern of public broadcasting. By applying the resource dependence model, it is possible to explain the Corporation for Public Broadcasting's responses to a dynamic external environment as well as the effects of decision outcomes on the implementation of public television policy. Therefore, the resource dependence model is used to evaluate the organizational performance of public television.

The data analyzed in this book cover fiscal years 1967 to 1989. Data were collected from archival records, observation, and interview. Archival records included congressional hearings documents, CPB legislative history, presidential documents, OMB memoranda, and CPB financial summaries and publications. House and Senate authorization hearings were observed. Congressional staff and CPB managers were interviewed. Interviews were also conducted with CPB and PBS officials, OMB budget examiners, and representatives of public television special interests groups. All interview respondents were promised anonymity. Throughout this book, their responses are designated by respondent (a randomly assigned number) and date of interview.

The impact of executive turnover and appropriations decision making is tracked through all levels—aggregate, agency, and lower—of public television organization over time. At the aggregate level, competing performance expectations held by dominant coalition decision participants—the executive, Congress, and the Corporation for Public Broadcasting—are examined. Special attention is given to the decision-making and budgetary structures of public television.

At the agency level, the effects of aggregate budgetary and policy outcomes on CPB internal management decision making—legislative tinkering—are described. Progressive increases in line item allocations to special interest groups within the public television industry who lobby Congress and the executive are presented. At the lower level of organization, the effects of these outcomes on the performance of public television are analyzed. Special attention is given to public television's attainment of the three primary goals identified in its mission statement: programming diversity, diversity in employment, and service to unserved and underserved audiences.

ORGANIZATION OF THE BOOK

The book is organized into seven chapters. In the first chapter, an overview of organizations theory is given. Two models of organizational behavior are introduced: the rational and resource dependence models. Definitions and indicators of organizational effectiveness are also presented for each model. In Chapter 2, a brief history of public television is provided. The culture of public television and the roles advocates and opponents play in the legal establishment of public broadcasting as a government-sponsored enterprise are described. The debate over the federal role in financing public broadcasting and its effectiveness as a public organization is also introduced.

In Chapter 3, the evolution of the organizational structure for the Corporation for Public Broadcasting is described; the definition of the mission of the Corporation is provided; and the other organizations that play leading roles in Corporation decision making are identified. For example, the Public Broadcasting Service, the entity established to interconnect public television stations, is identified and described. Also identified are the budgetary and decision-making structures imposed under four pivotal presidencies: Johnson, Nixon, Carter, and Reagan. In this chapter, public broadcasting policy and public television organization are shown to have been repeatedly redefined in accordance with the changing preferences and priorities that accompanied executive turnover.

An examination of the effects of executive turnover on the organization, strategic behavior, and performance of public television over time is continued in Chapter 4. The trade-offs that members of the public television industry make to ensure the survival of public broadcasting by compliance to the expectations of the dominant coalition members— the executive and Congress—are described. It is postulated that the Corporation's dependence upon increased appropriations and need to comply with executive and congressional preferences constrain public television policy. Herein, it is demonstrated that the search for survival— defined as increased and predictable budgetary appropriations—markedly alters strategic behavior and performance in public organizations.

In Chapter 5, the budgetary outcomes that result from executive turnover, the politics, and repeated reorganization encountered by the Corporation for Public Broadcasting in its search for survival, are described and explained. An analysis of budget outcomes and their impact on the CPB and lower levels of public television organization is undertaken to illustrate that control over public television organization and policy has been delegated progressively from agency administrators at the national level to station managers and other special interests groups at the lower level.

In Chapter 6, the effects of the budget-imposed policy shifts and aggregate budget outcomes on organizational performance at the lower levels of public television organization are evaluated. Three stated goals are given special attention: diversity in programming, diversity in employment, and service to underserved and unserved audiences. Herein, it is demonstrated that the organizational effectiveness of public television is constrained by both the political and budgetary uncertainty of the public broadcasting environment.

In conclusion, the preeminent question posed by this book is answered in Chapter 7: Is public television a panacea, pork barrel, or public trust? To make this assessment, the rational and resource dependence models of organizations theory are reconsidered because an accurate evaluation is contingent upon the behavioral explanations invoked by each model. In each model, assumptions and propositions are proffered that lead one to use different indicators, and thereby render divergent evaluations of organizational performance. The book is concluded with a discussion of the lessons to be learned from the Corporation for Public Broadcasting and the public policy implications for other public organizations.

NOTES

1. A public organization is any legislatively mandated organization, funded wholly or in part through the appropriations process, that provides a public service and performs an administrative function. This definition includes agencies, bureaus, quasi-government, and government-sponsored enterprises. See Scott, *Organizatons, Rational, Natural and Open Systems* (Englewood Cliffs: Prentice-Hall, 1981).

2. Ibid.

3. Although public radio is included in the Corporation's mission, only public television is the subject of this evaluation.

4. PL90–167.

5. Input is the procurement of resources required by the organization in order to carry out production functions. Throughput is the process of converting input into output—the execution of technical or production functions. Output is the outcome—what is produced.

PUBLIC TELEVISION

1

Organization Theory and the Public Organization

In all organizations, goal attainment—surviving and accomplishing the stated objectives or mission—has primacy. Although the public organization is certainly no exception to this rule, what is exceptional is that all too often managers of the public organization must trade off the attainment of stated goals in favor of survival goals. In private organizations, stated and survival goals can be sought simultaneously or sequentially as internal strategic management decisions. In the public organization, goal attainment is determined to a large extent by the politics of the federal budgetary process—the external environment. The very attributes that distinguish the public organization from all others—its legislative mandate and federal funding—also constrain performance.

During a period marked by disturbing and large federal deficits, most public policy analysts address the "crisis" of the federal budget process (Schick, 1985; White, 1988). In a market characterized by proliferative program requirements amid austerity, few look at the impact of this crisis on public organizations. Remarkably, even fewer look systematically at the effects of the increased competition for federal dollars on the structure, decision making, and goals of the public organization. Yet, whether and how the managers of public organizations cope with these constraints, and other partisan preferences imposed by the external environment, inform both public policy and generic organization theory.

However, some observers of public policy question the appropriateness and utility of a rigorous application of generic organization theory to public organizations, namely, Downs (1967); Rainey, Backoff, and Levine (1976); Bozeman (1987); and Gortner, Mahler, and Nicholson (1987). These authors assert that the present body of literature on organization theory virtually ignores fundamental differences between private and public organizations. They maintain the public organization's legal mandate and its dependence on the federal budget process make it distinctly different from the private organization.

Admittedly, the purpose of the budget process is to ensure resource inputs, so the public organization does not face an external market in the same way as the private organization (Downs, 1967). Whereas in the private organization, profit, which is determined directly by output, is synonymous with survival. Herein, goal attainment is the production of a highly demanded good at the lowest cost. Therefore, it is the strategic management of scarce resources that determines organizational effectiveness in the private organization.

Conversely, the public organization is confronted by a political market. Herein, organizational effectiveness is determined by adaptation to competing expectations for strategic behavior. In the public organization, one is unable to evaluate output in direct relation to the costs of input. For this reason, the absence of an external market or, more precisely, the presence of a political market has profound implications for performance in public organizations. Similarly, Gortner, Mahler, and Nicholson (1987) maintain that tremendous insight can be gained from the use of generic organization theory to explain decision outcomes in the public organization when that theory addresses the special and different qualities of the public organization—legislative mandate and federal funding.

In this chapter, these positions are discussed and the latter is substantiated. Generic organization theory is found to be inappropriate for the study of public organizations when it ignores these important differences and assumes that all organizations are essentially the same. Because the public organization is government-financed and legislatively mandated, it is more dependent upon political than economic markets for resources critical to survival. The public organization is dependent upon the mutual adjustment of a coalition of political institutions and actors, namely, the Executive Office of the President, the Office of Management and Budget, the Congress, and constituent groups for resource inputs and goals. As decision makers in the public organization negotiate the appropriations process, the competing policy preferences of these disparate interests with correspondingly disparate goals constrain goal attainment. The public organization's dependence upon this coalition of actors and its capacity to satisfy their competing expectations—more than rationally derived ends and means—determine organizational effectiveness.

In this chapter, the rational and resource-dependence models of organization theory are delineated in order to assess performance in the public organization. The utilization of the resource-dependence model is deemed more appropriate for the evaluation of public organizations than the rational model. Public television performance and, thereby, decision making in public organizations, that is, public policy, are proven to be constrained significantly by the reliance upon a disparate coalition that includes the executive, Congress, and a mixed public for the resources essential to production and performance. Partisan politics and the competing interests of coalition partners are proven to play principal roles in policy making to the extent that the structure and the very goals of the public organization are transformed over time. Consequently, an analysis of the decision-making outcomes that uses the resource dependence model of organization theory helps us better understand and make more generalizable predictions about the behavior of public organizations.

ORGANIZATION THEORY

Much of what we know about organizations comes largely as a byproduct of the search for improved organizational efficiency and performance undertaken by social scientists from different disciplines who hold one of two research perspectives about organizations. By imposing the closed system perspective, researchers assume that organizations are bounded and, thereby, determinate systems. The organization is reified as a rational actor that has complete control over its goals, structure, participants, and technology. Organizations are studied as if they are static and stable phenomena because the variables, and consequently uncertainty, are reduced (von Bertalanffy, 1950, 1956).

On the other hand, researchers ascribing to the natural systems perspective assume that organizations are open and responsive collectivities that exist within highly complex environments. The organization is seen as a set of interdependent networks or parts that together make up a whole because each contributes something and receives something from the whole, which in turn is interdependent with some larger environment (Thompson, 1967). According to the natural systems perspective, the organization is defined as a dynamic environment formed by a coalition of special interest groups with shared purposes. Herein, the organization is seen as adaptive, for no organization is so internally well-coordinated that all the resources critical to goal attainment—such as manpower, materials, and technology—can be secured solely by the internal application of sound management routines or standard operating procedures. Instead, the transactional relationships between the organization and its supporting environment—the interactions of input, throughput, and output—are central and to a large extent determine organizational behavior.

Both the closed system and open system strategies have produced a "theory of organizations" that is not a single theory tied together by a universal set of "truths."[1] Instead, the still nascent organization theory is comprised of competing constructs, multiple models, loosely coupled concepts, and profuse propositions. For example, organizations have been defined as formal bureaucracies with clear lines of authority (Weber, 1947; Durkheim, 1949; Michels 1962; Pareto, 1971); machines (Taylor, 1911); collectivities of small groups with informal norms (Lewin, 1948); rational or spontaneous entities (Gouldner, 1959); highly complex and structurally differentiated social associations (Blau, 1968, 1970); goal driven enterprises (Perrow, 1970); shifting coalitions (Cyert and March, 1963); organized anarchies (March and Olsen, 1976); resource dependent coalitions of specialized interests (Pfeffer and Salancik, 1978); as well as coordinated activity systems in pursuit of environmental niches (Aldrich, 1979).

Similarly, the decision-making process within such organizations is further characterized as wholly and purposively rational in search of optimal solutions (Weber, 1947; Pareto, 1971), boundedly rational in search of "satisficing" solutions (March and Simon, 1958); collectively bargained in search of conflict-reducing incremental solutions (Lindblom, 1959); garbage cans filled with accumulations of actors, problems, and solutions in search of a choice opportunity (Cohen, March, and Olsen, 1972); or coalitional in search of boundary spanning and resource-securing solutions (Pfeffer and Salancik, 1978).

THE RATIONAL MODEL

In this chapter, only two of these models are presented. The rational (classical) and resource dependence (environmental) models are used to explain the behavior and evaluate the effectiveness of public television. According to the rational model, organizations are viewed as if they are determinate systems composed of networks of actors with a common purpose in pursuit of clearly specified goals and means wherein the search for improved efficiency and optimal performance have primacy. Traditionally, all large, complex organizations—whether private or public—that exhibit these characteristics are said to be bureaucracies. Certain "bureaucratic" attributes arise from the rational model and customarily serve as the preconditions for effectiveness in all organizations.

Generally, the prototype for the rational model of organization is provided by Max Weber's work. Drawing largely from his studies of medieval trading companies and the Prussian Army, Weber's "ideal type" organization is the bureaucracy. The bureaucracy is a collectivity of social relationships purposively and rationally organized to execute social action. Rationality is the yardstick against which the institution and the individuals who constitute it are to be assessed. Just as the purpose is derived through rationality, the goals of the bureaucratic organization are also rationally derived. Goals are clear and explicit. Rules of behavior are written and there are standard procedures for organizational action. There is a division of labor with a pyramidal hierarchy of authority. Organizational tasks are divided, classified, and routinized. Lastly and importantly, the bureaucracy has an administrative staff that is separate from ownership, and officers are appointed on the basis of their competency.

Weber's rational–legal bureaucracy, as do all rational models, reifies organizational behavior and serves a utility function. Bureaucracies are said to behave like rational individuals. As organized collectivities for social action they specify well-defined goals, identify means that optimize goal attainment, and link means to ends as directly as possible. The organization exists as a system unto itself—closed—so goal attainment can be internally controlled. For the rational model, goals or ends reflect more than just output; they reflect internal organizational factors. Sound management practices and strategies, clear channels of communication and lines of authority, the division of labor, and the standardization of tasks are decided within the organization and determine performance. Under the rational model, limited attention is paid to external considerations because such factors are beyond the organization's direct control.

Therefore, the effective organization is defined as one that efficiently attains specified goals by directly controlling the linkage between ends and means. Efficient goal attainment is the production of a highly demanded good at the lowest cost. Output is evaluated in direct relation to input or, more explicitly, the profit margin. In the nongovernment organization, profitability determines survival and, thereby, effectiveness. For example, the manufacturing organization is evaluated in terms of the profits earned from the sale of goods after all production costs have been subtracted. Similarly, in the nonprofit human service organization, the attainment of goals clearly defined in the mission statement—usually accounted as units serviced within the limits of the budget—can be used to assess effectiveness.

The Rational Model and the Public Organization

How, then, does one evaluate effectiveness in the public organization from the rational perspective? Before one can offer a definitive answer to this question, one should determine whether the public organization exhibits the essential characteristics of the truly bureaucratic organization.

Although public organizations are generally called bureaucracies, not all public organizations are, in fact, bureaucracies in the strict sense.

Certainly, public organizations are large and complex. Public organizations have a division of labor with clearly delimited lines of authority or hierarchy. Administrative staff are not owners, and officers tend to be recruited on competency-based criteria. Rules of behavior are written and procedures for organizational behavior are standardized—standard operating procedures. However, this is where the preconditions of the rational model cease to be met in the public organization.

Typically, the purpose of the public organization is intentionally ill-defined, vague, or even obscure. Seldom are goals defined as rationally and explicitly as possible in the public organization. Instead, goals are deliberately defined as broadly as possible in order to encompass and minimally accommodate all interested groups and constituencies. In such a setting, one may be hard pressed to say that the search for improved efficiency and optimization of the linkage between ends and means has primacy. Input, throughput, and output are not subject initially or ultimately to internal control here. Rather, the public organization is dependent upon the external environment for its very creation, mission, maintenance, survival, and bottom line—the statement of profitability.

Despite these serious breaches with the rational model's preconditions, especially the rationality and clearly defined goal assumptions, many observers are predisposed to evaluate the public organization's effectiveness as though it was as rational, purposive, and internally controlled as the private organization.

This predisposition—one that is held by policy makers, managers, and analysts as well as constituency groups and students of organization theory alike—is examined in the following discussion. Moreover, it is the predisposition to evaluate public organizations as "bureaucratic" forms that leads some observers to conclude that public organizations are inherently inefficient and incapable of attaining any goals other than survival very effectively. From this analysis of public television decision behavior, one can advance two important propositions. First, use of the rational perspective causes one to invoke different criteria and employ, if not wholly inappropriate then certainly, less accurate yardsticks to assess effectiveness in public organizations. Second, the utilization of faulty indicators may lead one to draw false conclusions about the effectiveness of these organizations.

An Example: The Carnegie Task Force on Educational Television. In response to special interest advocacy for a protected environment, Congress commissioned two task forces on educational television, the first in 1966 and the second in 1978. In both Carnegie Commission reports on public television, task force members appear to have been guided by rational expectations for public television policy. Task force members defined clear and precise goals and means for the organization of public television. Entrusted with the task of implementing the 1927, 1934, and 1951 FCC and Comsat Acts, the first Carnegie Commission identified twelve recommendations for the creation, design, and maintenance of a public organization for educational television.[2] Covering all facets of public television operation, the recommendations of the first Carnegie Commission maximally linked the diverse goals of the various groups interested in the establishment and maintenance of a national system of educational television. The recommendations defined both the organizational structure and financing for educational television. Structured as a modified pyramid type of hierarchy and financed by means of an excise tax on the sale of television sets, the first Carnegie Commission proposed a "Public Television Corporation" with clearly delimited lines of authority, optimal goals, and politically insulated means.[3]

In spite of their logic and rationality, the Carnegie Commission recommendations were not followed fully. Other considerations and priorities of the Johnson Administration were woven into the public broadcasting bill. Threatened opposition from the manufacturers of television sets and potential objection from Congress were averted by the deletion of the two key funding provisions. In the interest of avoiding opposition from television set manufacturers, the clause that recommended the financing of public television from revenues generated by an excise tax on the sale of television sets was removed.

In the interest of circumventing likely objections from Mr. Wilbur Mills (D-AK), then Chairman of the House Ways and Means Committee, the provision for long-term financing, which would have set an appropriations precedent, was omitted. President Lyndon B. Johnson deemed it difficult, if not impossible, to fulfill his promise of long-range financing for a national system of public television. Given the cost overruns of the Vietnam War, the President concluded that the "time was not ripe for long-term insulated financing."[4]

President Johnson, anticipating an adverse response by commercial broadcasters and Congress to the Carnegie recommendations, proposed a compromise public broadcasting bill. The 1967 Public Broadcasting Act provided funding through the federal appropriations process. In addition, two provisions of the "Great Society" legislation were inserted into the 1967 Public Broadcasting Act: expanded educational opportunity and minority hiring. Public broadcasting was further mandated to provide high-quality and diverse programming for hitherto underserved or unserved television audiences. Also included in the 1967 Act was a provision for the development of public radio—an issue that the first Carnegie Commission had not addressed.

Although the rationally derived Carnegie recommendations linked means to ends and may have been optimal, they were not adopted as proposed. Some adjustment to external considerations was necessary.

What was at issue, here, was not the application of the optimal solution to the problem of "what to do with public broadcasting in America," but the application of a solution satisfactory to the executive, Congress, constituencies, and special interest groups concerned with public broadcasting (Carnegie Commission, 1967). Consequently, the 1967 Act, further detached the goals of educational television from their optimal means by providing funding for public broadcasting through the federal budgetary process. Public broadcasting was rendered vulnerable to powerful political actors, special interest groups, and the economic fortunes or misfortunes of other public organizations for input, throughput, and output. In short, the organization of public television had been made more dependent upon political markets than economic ones.

To the question of how effectively does public television accomplish its goals, one may respond: extremely poorly, moderately well, or very well. Indeed, the most appropriate response is contingent upon the particular point in time, the specific goal or goals, as well as the organizational perspective. To a great extent, the harsh criticism often hurled at public television reflects the application of inappropriate criteria used to evaluate its organizational effectiveness more than the poor performance of this public organization over time.

THE RESOURCE DEPENDENCE MODEL

Before venturing further speculation on the question of public television's accomplishment of stated goals, let us consider the resource dependence model of organizational behavior. This model gives more insightful and useful explanations of behavior in the public organization because it rests squarely upon external considerations of the organization's situation of dependence. The focus of the resource dependence model is on the organization's responses to the external environment. The model is an application of Emerson's (1962) power dependence construct.

A depends upon B if he aspires to goals or gratifications whose achievement is facilitated or hindered by appropriate actions on B's part. By virtue of mutual dependency, it is more or less imperative to each party that he be able to control or influence the other's conduct. . . . Ties of mutual dependence imply that each party is in a position to grant or deny, facilitate or hinder, the other's gratification. The power to control or influence the other resides in control over the things he values, e.g., [from] oil resources to ego support, depending upon the relation in question.[5]

Several researchers have refined this approach. Thompson (1967) and Jacobs (1974) have called it the power dependence model. Zald and

Wamsley (1973) have entitled their version political economy. However, Pfeffer and Salancik (1978) have presented the most comprehensive discussion of this model. These authors emphasize the primacy of the organization's linkages to its environment and the external control exercised by networks upon which the organization is resource dependent. They define the organization as a network of coalitions that alters its purposes and domains to regulate transactions, and, thereby, stabilizes the flow of resources and accommodates new interests. The effective organization is the environmentally responsive organization. The environmentally responsive organization is one that adjusts to the demands of networks within its environment in accordance with its dependence upon the resources supplied by those networks. Consequently, the survival and, ultimately, the success of an organization are determined by the organization's awareness of its environment and the manner in which it enacts that environment (ibid., 84).

Because public organizations are environments enacted through law and social sanction, they are the instruments of public policy. Public organizations—such as the Corporation for Public Broadcasting—are protected environments that result from the organized efforts of networks of specialized interests to achieve common policy preferences. Trade associations, corporations, church and neighborhood groups, professional bodies, etc., form coalitions, and then lobby government leadership to create, through legislative mandate, an environment that ensures their policy preferences are met (ibid.). The political market, that is, the appropriations process, becomes the place for formally institutionalizing the survival of the public organization by guaranteeing access to the resources it needs to carry out that mandate.

Pfeffer and Salancik (1978) further maintain that mutual dependence (interdependence) and its management are essential to goal attainment. Both are key concepts in the resource dependence model. These authors build upon Emerson's power construct and maintain that social relations engender ties of mutual dependence between parties. One organization's output is the other's input, and vice versa. Therefore, parties strive to alter these interdependencies in order to regulate the transactions—flows of resources across boundaries—and make them more predictable.

Given the complexity of modern society, few, if any, organizations can incorporate all the resources required for output within themselves as Parsons (1956) suggests in the rational model. The focal organization must deliberately manipulate its relations with other organizations or actors in order to guarantee the supply of resources critical to output. These relations or exchanges with the environment take place at the boundaries of the organization, where the control over individuals, activities, and other organizations diminishes. Because mutual dependence characterizes the nature of the exchange, it also generates uncertainty about the predictability and stability of the resource exchange (Pfeffer and Salancik, 1978).

The Resource Dependence Model and the Public Organization

In an uncertain environment, managers of the resource dependent organization must develop alternative resource suppliers in order to secure steady flows of critical resources and, thereby, reduce dependence (Thompson, 1967; Pfeffer and Salancik, 1978). Because the stable and predictable resource exchange assures organizational survival, uncertainty, or instability with respect to important resources threatens the continued existence of the organization. When a resource is scarce and essential to survival, the organization is more compliant with the supplier's demands for reciprocity—payment. In exchange for stable and predictable flows of resources, the public organization must comply with the expectations and demands of Congress, the executive, and special interest groups—collectively, the coalition partners.

Compliance. Empirical studies by Aharoni (1971) and Salancik (1976) provide compelling evidence that organizations are more compliant when they are resource dependent. In his study of Israeli managers, Aharoni (1971) found that firms most reliant upon government financing were also most compliant with government requests and employment policies. When general managers of 141 of Israel's largest manufacturers were asked whether they would be willing to forego investment options in favor of investment in a development area designated by the government with assured earnings of a fixed percentage, firms selling a larger proportion of their output to the government were willing to give up larger yields from investment elsewhere in order to comply with the government's requests. Similarly, Salancik (1976), in his study of defense contractors and hiring, found a high correlation between the degree of organizational dependence on government business and their enforcement of affirmative action guidelines.[6]

Both studies suggest that the stable and effective organization is one that satisfies the demands of its critical resource suppliers. Other research on the relationship between resource dependence and compliance also indicates that the effective organization strives to alter its reliance on a single supplier in order to reduce dependence and the need for compliance. Thompson (1967), Randall (1973), and Pfeffer (1972) maintain that the effective organization concomitantly seeks to decrease its reliance on a single critical source of supply while it stabilizes the flow of critical resources.

Coalition Formation. From the array of coalition partners who enact the public organization comes competing and disparate demands, priorities, and criteria for organizational performance. Unlike the private organization, in the public organization, typically, the coalition actors agree only on the need for a policy, not on the instrument itself. Therefore, effectiveness in the public organization and, ultimately, survival are greatly constrained by that very network that coalesces to enact it.

Consequently, coalition formation emerges as an important factor in the study of organizational behavior because it plays three salient roles in the public organization. First, coalition formation permits both organizational enactment and the management of interdependence through the appropriations process. Second, it serves as an indicator of organizational effectiveness or performance. The very existence of the public organization implies that members of the coalition are satisfied with its performance to the extent that coalition partners remain active and supportive of the organization. Third, organizational survival dictates keeping interest groups on board and maintaining their happiness or satisfaction by means of compliance to performance demands.

However, competing demands among coalition participants can pose problems to survival as the organization attempts to secure scarce resources and simultaneously sustain the coalition of support needed for operation. Should the demands of coalition partners fail to be met sufficiently, one can expect dissatisfied partners to abandon ship. Should coalition partners exit in sufficient numbers or exit with irreplaceable resources, one should then expect the organization to die.

Survival and Organizational Effectiveness. Organizational effectiveness can then be defined as the public organization's ability to create actions and outcomes acceptable to the coalition partners. In this way, organizational effectiveness is an external standard of performance that reflects how well an organization meets the demands of its environment. Because organization participants come into the coalition when there are benefits or advantages to be gained and exit when they perceive no advantage to be gained from the interactions (Hirschman, 1970; Pfeffer and Salancik, 1978), the stable participation of interest groups, the distribution of benefits to those groups over time, and compliance with performance demands of resource suppliers should be valid and reliable indicators of organizational effectiveness.

Budgetary growth over time emerges as an indicator of effectiveness in the public organization. Budgetary growth reflects the organization's ability to derive the resources required for production from the environment by satisfactory performance. The public organization, as an environment enacted by law and social sanction, is dependent upon federal appropriations. Federal appropriations are transactions regulated by Congress and the executive in collaboration with presidentially appointed caretakers of these environments—the agency officials. Increased appropriations constitute budgetary growth and, thereby, are indicative of organizational effectiveness.

Given their centrality to the appropriations process, Congress and the executive are the dominant members of the coalition charged to act on behalf of the other coalition partners, which includes trade associations, industry professionals, community groups, and interested individuals. Accountability and compliance to congressional and executive policy preferences, priorities, and expectations supersede those of coalition members who supply resources deemed more marginal to the public organization. Therefore, compliance to official interpretations of the public organization's legislative mandate rather than profits secured from the marketability and quality of its product determines, to a significant degree, the public organization's budget appropriation and, thereby, its survival.

By virtue of its dependence upon the federal budgetary process as the primary resource supplier and the subsequent need to comply with the demands of this supplier, the public organization's discretion and autonomy are greatly diminished. Because the legislative and executive branches concertedly act as the principal supplier of a single critical resource—dollars—the public organization becomes most compliant with the demands of these dominant coalition participants. As managers of the public organization seek stable and predictable monetary flows from Congress in order to survive, their capacity to make decisions and carry them out is greatly constrained. In this respect, the public organization is far more vulnerable to successful influence attempts than the private organization.

Over time, resource dependence and political vulnerability erode the public organization's discretion and autonomy such that this loss generally culminates in goal dilution.[7] Goal dilution occurs when organizational survival supersedes successful attainment of the mission, and the organization becomes the end instead of the means. Managers pursue only those activities that engender sustained support for the existence of the organization itself. Should certain organizational pursuits be unsatisfactory to the resource supplier, despite their appropriateness to the task, they may be altered or discontinued altogether. Therefore, the dependence upon a single critical resource supplier and compliance with the expectations of that supplier have profound implications for behavior in public organizations.

SUMMARY

Organization theory greatly enhances our knowledge of behavior in public organizations. More specifically, the resource dependence model better explains public policy making. Using this model, we see that all organizations—especially public ones—are coalitions that alter their goals, means, and domains in order to secure resources critical to survival. In this model, we view all organizations as dynamic, adaptive to their external environments, as well as purposive. By using the resource dependence model, indicators can be derived that take into account organizational responsiveness to the external environment in addition to the internally derived definitions of optimal means and rational ends. Organization theory also suggests that the researcher examine the linkage between the organization and its external environment in order to provide more insightful explanations and accurate evaluations of organizational effectiveness. Public organizations are externally controlled and thus more subject to the vagaries of political markets than economic ones. Therefore, the imposition of the resource dependence model greatly facilitates the analysis of behavior in public organizations.

In the balance of this book, a description is given of the culture, organization, and performance of public television under the administration of the Corporation for Public Broadcasting. Compliance with the policy expectations of the executive and Congress, in order to survive as an entity, is shown to emerge as a primary goal, superseding even the need to deliver the product sought by other members of the coalition who lobby for its creation and continuation. Politics and executive turnover—with their attendant alterations to policy—are shown to constrain organizational structure, decision making, and autonomy to the extent that the very mission of the public organization is diluted over time.

The assessment of public television's organizational effectiveness that follows will inform both students of generic organization theory and public administrators about the behavior of public organizations. In the remaining chapters, the history of Corporation for Public Broadcasting (CPB) decision behavior from inception to 1989 is explicated, from an idea shared by a coalition of specialized interest groups to its enactment and present status as a government-sponsored enterprise. The reader will discern that once enacted, the situation of legally mandated resource dependence upon the federal budgetary process exerts enormous influence on organizational effectiveness.

NOTES

1. See Harold Gortner, Julianne Mahler, and Jeanne Nicholson, *Organizational Theory: A Public Perspective* (Chicago: Dorsey Press, 1987).

2. See Appendix for the specific recommendations and hierarchy.

3. See George H. Gibson, *Public Broadcasting* (New York: Praeger, 1977), and Carnegie Commission Report, *A Public Trust* (New York: Bantam, 1979).

4. See Carnegie Commission Report, *Public Television: A Program for Action* (New York: Bantam, 1967).

5. Richard M. Emerson, "Power Dependence Relations," *American Sociological Review*, 27 (1962): 23.

6. $R = 0.89$; see Pfeffer and Salancik, *The External Control of Organizations* (New York: Harper and Row, 1978, p. 57), and Yair Aharoni, *The Israeli Manager* (Tel Aviv: Tel Aviv University, 1971).

7. A concept first proffered in a treatise on political organizations by Robert Michels, *Political Parties* (New York: The Free Press, 1962). Goal dilution is now accepted as descriptive of goal-directed behavior in a variety of organizations, particularly public ones.

2

Building a Coalition for Public Television

Panacea, pork barrel, or public trust? Some twenty-odd years after its inception and still struggling with an identity crisis, public broadcasting continues to flounder as a public organization. Like all public organizations, the mission and record of public broadcasting are the subjects of some scrutiny at regular intervals. Unlike most public organizations and in spite of its broad policy appeal, however, public television as the dominant entity of the Corporation for Public Broadcasting continues to undergo massive structural, discretionary, and budgetary revision.

In this chapter, an explanation is offered to show how an organization can experience as much budgetary growth as public television, yet be the object of such salient criticism on its record of organizational performance. In service to many varied interests over the years, some supporters believe that public broadcasting, and specifically public television, has failed to fulfill some important goals in its legislative mandate. Some wonder whether public television has moved from being a panacea for a public interested in the medium's educational uses to functioning as a pork barrel for public television industry professionals, and whether it is even capable of serving the "public" interest.[1]

Usually around the time for authorization hearings, articles appear in various print media that highlight the progress and problems of public broadcasting. However, the recently past twentieth anniversary of public broadcasting brought a spate of the harshest criticism and most far-flung headlines ever penned. Articles appeared ranging from "Highbrow Pork Barrel" (*Washington Post*, 8/16/87), "Public Television: Can It Survive" (*TV Guide*, 8/1/87), "Why It's Time for Public TV to Go Private" (*New York Times*, 11/1/87), "For Something Completely Cheap" (*Harpers*, 11/

87), and "Paradise Postponed" (*Channels*, 9/87) to "Public Broadcasters Looking for a Sure Thing" (*Broadcasting*, 11/16/87).

In addition to the recurrent funding issue, these articles question the policies, performance, viability, and the very feasibility of public broadcasting. Observers, critics, and advocates concur that, as an organization, public broadcasting is in dire need of overhaul. Deemed by some as a "poverty program for the well to do," by others a "country club for broadcasting professionals," and by still others as "overly cautious," "a name without a concept," and "safely splendid," all agree that public broadcasting has consistently failed to cope with some serious organizational problems. Citing Congress's failure to provide long-range federal funding, ongoing political interference, and failure to take programming risks, some formerly ardent advocates assert that public broadcasting has not lived up to its potential. All, essentially, charge that despite significant budgetary growth, public broadcasting has failed to attain its mission to

encourage noncommercial educational radio and television broadcast programming which will be responsive to the interests of the people both in particular localities and throughout the United States, and which will constitute an expression of diversity and excellence; (PL 90–129) [and] increase public telecommunications services and facilities available to, operated by, and owned by minorities and women; (PL 95–567).

CULTURE OF PUBLIC TELEVISION

In order to formulate an appropriate answer to the fundamental question posed by this book, first, it is necessary to review the origins of public television. The literature on public broadcasting, mass media, and economic regulation describes the evolution of a policy that is dynamic, complex, and anarchic yet rich with promise. Most notably Barnouw (1966); Coase (1969); Noll, Peck, and McGowan (1973); Smith (1973); Gans (1974); Macy (1974); Guimary (1975); Gibson (1977); and Blakeley (1979) characterize the development of both commercial and noncommercial broadcasting as piecemeal and industry-driven. According to these analysts, the Corporation for Public Broadcasting is the product of free enterprise forces and government intervention in the broadcasting market.

Impetus for a national system of educational television arose from a culture characterized by tremendous technological innovation in telecommunications, the economic and educational potential of the new medium, postwar factors, and Great Society liberalism (Smith, 1973; Macy, 1974; Gibson, 1977; and Blakeley, 1979). Like most inventions, the development of a national system of public television was haphazard and serendipitous. The early advocates of public television held very disparate and often ill-defined goals for the enterprise. The telecommunications industry, university educators, and philanthropic foundations constituted the core coalition of special interest groups that actively lobbied Congress and the executive to federally fund public television.

So-called "public" participation in broadcasting was manifest largely at the whim of the commercial networks to provide guidance to sponsors in their efforts to increase audience share and, thereby, product profitability for programs sponsored by advertising (Guimary, 1975). To this end, "citizen councils" were established to advise broadcasters on programming and marketing strategies. Although the "public" was seen by the commercial networks as homogeneous and ancillary in its early years, the rise of consumerism in the 1960s has shown that public television's "public" has been, and remains, quite diverse (Rowland, 1976; Guimary, 1975; Frank and Greenberg, 1982; and Grossman, 1988). In this chapter, we discern that the only purpose commonly shared by all proponents was that some system of educational (subsequently designated public) television be created by the federal government to provide the educational, informational, and cultural programming that commercial broadcasters considered unprofitable.

The roots of public television rest in radio, which was the only form of broadcasting before the public debut of television at the 1939 World's Fair. Prior to World War I, the use of radio was largely unregulated and limited to point-to-point communications by governmental, military, mostly amateur, and a few commercial operators (Network Project, 1971; Gibson, 1977; and Blakeley, 1979). Station licenses were granted to any U.S. citizen or company that applied and met the legal requirements.[2] Licenses were held predominantly by amateur radio broadcasters. These included institutional, university physics and engineering faculty, and student broadcasters. Few had any inkling of the veritable gold mine broadcasting would become. With the wartime ban on transmitters removed and the entry of commercial broadcasters underway, by 1923, the number of amateur broadcasters would thin substantially. To this technological innovation that amateurs had only tinkered with, both World Wars brought significant alterations. Radio licensure, spectrum allocation, market dynamics, coverage, and usage were all dramatically increased.[3]

After World War I, telecommunications manufacturers greatly accelerated and expanded their research, development, and marketing activities in radio. The supply demands of World War II resulted in a newsprint shortage, which generated a concomitant avalanche of radio advertising and, thereby, produced unanticipated revenue for the fledgling commercial radio stations (Guimary, 1975, p. 31). A few manufacturers foresaw the benefits to be gained from broadcasting and diversified into commercial networks to increase the sale of radios and advertising. The First Amendment enabled market forces to create institutions of broadcasting and to process their products. The American listener was identified as the purchaser of the receiving set. The listener was thus an extension of the phonograph purchaser and the revenue of radio was derived from the sales of sets (Smith, 1971, p. 73).

Foremost, both World Wars brought recognition of the power of the medium and its most profound use: mass manipulation through propaganda (Network Project, 1971; Gans, 1974; and Blakeley, 1979). "Only later was the discovery made that broadcasting was the most powerful 'selling' instrument hitherto devised" by the realization that public opinion could be shaped by politically organized campaigns of mass persuasion (Blakeley, 1979). Fears of sedition and censorship in the aftermath of the Korean War and McCarthyism spurred leaders from all sectors of American society to explore and develop educational and cultural uses for the broadcast media. Under President Lyndon Johnson's Administration, these events, innovations, and uses would culminate in the enactment of legislation to ensure a protected environment for the positive use of television on the public's behalf: the Corporation for Public Broadcasting.

The Federal Role in Public Broadcasting

In 1927, Congress empowered the Federal Radio Commission to issue licenses to radio stations that served the "public interest, necessity, or convenience." However, recognition of the need for a national system of noncommercial broadcasting was first recorded in the federal budget as the Communications Act of 1934. This public law transferred licensure and extended regulatory powers to the Federal Communications Commission (FCC). Officials of this new entity also allocated frequencies for commercial use, provided guidelines for commercial licensure and regulation, and commissioned a study for the reservation of channels for noncommercial use in the "public interest" (Coase, 1969; Blakeley, 1979).

In an early effort to provide guidelines for the new industry, the FCC published *Public Service Responsibility of Broadcast Licensees* in 1946. In the so-called "Blue Book," licensees were urged to "avoid advertising excesses," and license renewal was made contingent upon compliance with the "Fairness Doctrine." The Fairness Doctrine required broadcast licensees to:

(1) satisfactorily maintain an overall program balance, (2) provide time for programs inappropriate for sponsorship, (3) provide time for programs serving particular minority tastes and interests, (4) provide time for nonprofit organi-

zations, and (5) provide time for experiment and unfettered artistic self-expression (FCC, 1946, p. 55).

In 1951, under the leadership of FCC Commissioner Freda B. Hennock, the 1934 Communications Act was amended so that 80 VHF (very high-frequency) and 162 UHF (ultrahigh-frequency) channels were reserved for educational use. In 1958, equipment grants of $1 million per state were made to educational television stations. Two pivotal additions to this burgeoning body of communications legislation were made in 1962. The Communications Satellite Act established a public–private corporation for the operation of an international satellite relay system to provide global interconnection with the capacity for simultaneous and live transmission, which educational broadcasters had long sought and also benefitted commercial broadcasters.[4] The other bill, known as the Educational Facilities Act of 1962 and administered by HEW's Office of Education, provided $32 million dollars in matching funds as facilities grants to establish and maintain noncommercial educational television stations.

Taken collectively, these acts resulted from the usually concerted and occasionally competitive activity of special interest groups. Broadcasting special interest groups included visionaries from higher education, telecommunications manufacturers, private philanthropy, and government, who anticipated the economic and social potential of the broadcast media. Passage of these bills greatly facilitated the development and integration of communications technology and, thereby, expanded the growth and profits of the telecommunications industry. Manufacturers and commercial broadcasters would obtain phenomenal profits from the sale of communications equipment, radio and television sets, and especially advertising broadcast over the public's airwaves on frequencies freely licensed by the government because they served the public interest by educating and entertaining its citizenry.

Advocates of Public Television

Educational and Commercial Broadcasters. As early as 1925, a group of educational radio broadcasters, in anticipation of both the increased demand for allocations of a finite broadcast spectrum and the educational potential of these media, formed the Association of College and University Broadcasting Stations (ACUBS), the parent organization of the National Association of Educational Broadcasters (NAEB).[5] This group actively lobbied government officials, including the FCC, for the reservation of channels for noncommercial use and the development of a national noncommercial program exchange or interconnection capability. By 1940, its efforts had secured the reservation of five FM stations.

By 1945, the number of FM stations had increased to 20 (Gibson, 1977, p. 54; Blakeley, 1979, p. 72).

Corporations most responsive to the technological innovations within the industry included Westinghouse Electric and Manufacturing Corporation, owner of the heterodyne circuit used in radio receivers; General Electric, preeminent in the transoceanic communications market; and American Telephone and Telegraph (AT&T), which primarily was concerned with exploiting its exclusive monopoly of long distance telephone lines.

Continued technological advancement and speculation in the telecommunications industry culminated in the formation of the commercial networks (Noll, Peck, and McGowan, 1973; Gibson, 1977; Blakeley, 1979). Radio Corporation of America (RCA), formed in 1919, was an alliance of General Electric, AT&T, Western Electric, and the Marconi Wireless Company. In 1926, RCA became the National Broadcasting Company (NBC), after AT&T divested itself of RCA shares over a dispute about wire and wireless telegraphy and telephony. The Columbia Broadcasting System (CBS) was founded in 1927 and sold advertising to sustain itself. The American Broadcasting Company (ABC) was formed when Edward Noble purchased NBC's "Blue" network in 1943 (Blakely, 1979, p. 4; Noll, Peck, and McGowan, 1973).

Spurred by the desire to capitalize on the increased sophistication of communications technology and to expand markets, the telecommunications industry, in addition to its in-house initiatives, also greatly stimulated and subsidized university experimentation in broadcasting during this period. Largely by funneling funds through the engineering departments of major universities, corporations ensured the continued research and development of radio and television. As a consequence, most educational stations were licensed to state universities and operated by electronics faculty, who encouraged their students to tinker with the new technology. Commercial broadcasters remained ardent supporters of educational broadcasting as long as it filled the research-and-development void created when commercial broadcasters pursued the more lucrative activities afforded by these media.

Because of its commitment to the dissemination of knowledge and role in the refinement of broadcast technology as well as the alleged marginal returns afforded by educational productions, educational broadcasting was viewed as the preferred producer of high-quality cultural, educational, and public affairs programs. So the early years of broadcasting were marked by a general pattern of cooperation between educational and commercial broadcasting.

With encouragement and occasional direct funding support and commitments to air informational programs from commercial broadcasting, educational broadcasting typically provided the prototypes for public affairs productions in both radio and television (Blakeley, 1979, p. 8). For example, the Sloan Foundation financed the highly regarded University of Chicago radio production, *The University of Chicago Round Table*. This program introduced the format for "the radio talk show" and was carried by commercial stations nationwide, and in Canada, from 1931–1955. Between 1951 and 1955, the critically acclaimed *Omnibus*, produced by the Ford Foundation-funded Television–Radio Workshop, was aired regularly during prime time, initially on CBS and later on ABC.

Only when the commercial networks viewed themselves as competing with each other for audience shares and advertising or competing with educational broadcasters for scarce spectrum space (e.g., the reservation of channels) and technical capacity (e.g., satellite interconnection) has there been friction between these two segments of the industry. Again, *Omnibus* serves as a good example. Despite its numerous citations for excellence and trail-blazing production techniques, *Omnibus* was dropped by the commercial networks, first CBS and then ABC, when they chose to compete with each other for larger audience shares and advertising dollars.

Commercial broadcasters and telecommunications manufacturers respond with outright opposition to educational broadcasting when a conflict of interests is perceived on legislative initiatives such as the reservation of channels and interconnection. Given the adverse response by commercial broadcasters to these initiatives particularly, and the ever-diminishing air time allocated for their productions, educational broadcasters have gradually assumed a more prominent role in the development of more reliable alternative mechanisms for the distribution and transmission of informational and cultural programming. After 1949, educational broadcasters, persuaded by the strident exhortations of the foundations, actively advocated legislation for the reservation of channels and the development of a national system of interconnection (Network Project, 1971; Blakeley, 1979, p. 117).

Philanthropy. The Ford and Carnegie foundations have been most instrumental in the funding, development, and institutionalization of public broadcasting (Schramm and Nelson, 1972; Ford Foundation, 1976; Gibson, 1977; Blakeley, 1979).[6] Foremost, Ford Foundation initiatives in broadcasting led to the reservation of channels for educational use and the development of the model still used to activate, finance, and program educational television stations. Propelled by the desire to increase international market share and to quell the atmosphere of fear and suspicion in the wake of World War II, the Korean War, and McCarthyism, managers of the Ford Motor Corporation saw the power and potential of the broadcast media in education, especially television.[7]

In 1951, a financially enhanced Ford Foundation launched two historic and unprecedented educational projects in mass communications: the

Fund for Adult Education and the Fund for the Advancement of Education. Both charitable subsidiaries sought to utilize the innovation of television in the attainment of the Ford Foundation's overall mission "to contribute to the development of mature, wise, and responsible citizens who can participate intelligently in a free society (Blakely, 1979, p. 84)." The Fund for Adult Education (FAE) was concerned with the use of television in informal adult education, whereas the latter project was concerned with the formal education of youth in the elementary grades through the college level.

For ten years, both entities steadfastly strove to make educational television a reality—as the Fourth Network (Network Project, 1971; Pepper, 1979). While the Fund for the Advancement of Education embarked on an ambitious program of research into the effects of viewing television and its instructional uses, the Fund for Adult Education identified three critical goals geared to the organization of educational television as a government-sponsored enterprise:

1.) To secure the reservation of channels for educational television by the FCC. 2.) To encourage and assist educators in the activation of new stations through funding, training, and leadership. 3.) To create a national educational television center for the exchange of programs, ideas, information, and services.[8]

To achieve these aims, the FAE commenced a campaign to coopt those special interest groups already involved in educational broadcasting by direct financial investment in their organizations and projects, the provision of consultative services, and the creation of new television enterprises as they were needed (Network Project, 1971, p. 6). The Ford Foundation made grants to broadcasting institutions, facilities, professional and trade associations, and provided direct employment to academics, station engineers, educational broadcasters, and lay persons on Ford-initiated projects.

For example, through a five-year program of generous grantsmanship, FAE progressively assumed financial control over several educational broadcasting organizations including the American Council on Education (ACE), the Joint Council on Educational Television (JCET), and the National Association of Educational Broadcasters (NAEB). The FAE also established two pivotal production facilities: the Educational Television and Radio Center (ETRC) and National Educational Television (NET). The Ford Foundation's FAE even created a citizens council, the National Citizens Committee for Educational Television (NCET). In the future, Ford Foundation goals for a Fourth Network and its heavy-handed methods would place it in conflict with the Corporation for Public Broadcasting and retard the operation of its interconnection entity, the Public

Broadcasting Service (Network Project, 1971, p. 12; Blakeley, 1979; Pepper, 1983).

Conversely, the role of most other philanthropies involved with the institutionalization of public television was primarily advisory. For example, the Rockefeller Foundation funded two early meetings, the Allerton House Seminars, that defined the purposes of educational broadcasting in 1949 and 1950 (Gibson, 1977, p. 79; Blakeley, 1979, p. 10). Similarly, the Carnegie Corporation financed studies and conferences whose objectives were to establish and expand educational broadcasting as a distinct and insulated industry. From its support of the Wilbur Advisory Committee on Education by Radio in 1929 and its establishment of the highly acclaimed Commissions on Educational Television (*Public Television: A Program for Action* and *The Future of Public Broadcasting*) to the underwriting of *Sesame Street*, the Carnegie Foundation has acted chiefly as a facilitator in the development of public television.

Public Participation. Thus far, the discussion has identified only the. philanthropic entities and the clientele groups within the telecommunications industry who have been most instrumental in the legal enactment of public television. Now let us turn our attention to the public's role.

"Public" involvement in broadcasting has been uneven. Throughout most of radio and television's on-the-air history, the public—like the audience—has been regarded as homogeneous and ancillary. Only with the advent of a climate of consumerism and citizen participation in the late 1960s would this perception change. According to Donald Guimary (1975), the public has played only a minor role in the development of public television and this role has been scripted largely by the broadcast media, principal proponents for the creation of a government entity for educational television.

Prior to the 1960s, citizen groups active in broadcasting represented a narrow spectrum of American life. Formed mainly by middle and upper-class persons who were associated with civic and service associations and interested in radio, broadcasting councils were first recorded in 1922 (Guimary, 1975, p. 31). With encouragement from the FCC, the commercial networks and the National Association of Broadcasters (NAB) supported the formation of citizen councils to advise radio broadcasters. Representatives from membership groups such as the General Federation of Women's Clubs, the National PTA, and the National Council of Churches served on the citizen councils for broadcasting. Usually, the objectives of the citizen councils were developed and articulated by the commercial networks themselves. For example, in 1950, NBC devised guidelines for citizen participation that included coordination of "the interests of civic, religious and educational and business organizations

. . . patronage for sponsors of radio programs . . . aid parents in assuming responsibility for children's radio . . . [and] to develop recommendations to radio stations of standards deemed to be desirable for broadcasting in the public interest, convenience, and necessity."[9]

By 1947, however, the NAB—and by 1977, the CPB—would reverse its policy that encouraged and enlisted citizen participation in broadcasting. During World War II, the newsprint shortage gave way to an advertising surplus in radio. Newspapers were compelled to turn away advertising given the limited space. Consequently, many businesses shifted to radio advertising. Furthermore, the war generated excess profits that corporations diverted to radio advertising in order to decrease their tax burdens. This so-called advertising avalanche led the broadcasting industry to conclude that it had come of age and no longer needed to enlist or support groups to promote itself and its sponsors (Guimary, 1975, p. 33). From 1947 until the increased awareness of consumers about the use of public resources in the early 1970s, public participation in broadcasting would remain restricted largely to the criticism of television violence and its harmful effects on youth.

Neither homogenous nor expendable, public television's viewing audience is quite diverse. In a study commissioned by the CPB, Frank and Greenburg (1982) identified the public television market as comprised of News and Information, Family Integrated Activities, Highly Diversified, and Arts and Culture audience segments. Typically, these have been higher socioeconomic status audiences. Quite ironically, the CPB has exploited its special interest audience representation by eschewing the goal of reaching large audience collectivities in favor of a cumulatively larger and loyal following composed of smaller and more diversified, that is, specialized audiences.

This perspective differs dramatically from that of commercial ratings services like Arbitron and A. C. Nielsen Company that, until recent years, have viewed the audience in mass society terms, aggregated and undifferentiated (Smith, 1973; Guimary, 1975). These companies are more concerned with head counts of the total number of persons that watch a particular program during prime time on a given night. (In the early days, demographics was the province of marketing departments in advertising agencies who pitched their ads to specific income groups.)

The Role of the Special Interest Groups. As did the managers of commercial networks, CPB administrators also defined the role, nature, and extent of public participation in noncommercial broadcasting. Although the 1967 Carnegie Commission on public television recommended the formation of a national advisory citizens council to provide policy advice, as a CPB-created entity, the Advisory Council of National Organizations (ACNO) largely served as a lobby device for whipping up popular and legislative support at the Corporation's behest. Formed in 1969 to win popular support for public broadcasting, ACNO has consisted of as many as 78 national organizations such as the PTA, the American Bar Association, NAACP, AFL–CIO, NEA, and the United States Jaycees. In September 1977, with CPB approval, ACNO voted for dissolution because it had ceased to be a truly advisory and public forum for public broadcasting and had degenerated into a rhetorical device for the CPB.[10]

Aside from the highly orchestrated participation of clientele groups within the industry and representatives from national membership organizations cultivated by public broadcasters, the definition of public television's public remains obscure. In the words of one broadcasting analyst, Willard Rowland, public television's publics are

Scattered as audiences, and ignored as potentially active, creative partners in a public communications endeavor, noncommercial broadcasting publics have been and remain unaware of their rights and potentialities in the formulation of policy for the control and funding of the enterprise.

Not surprisingly, many public broadcasting administrators are not overly anxious to change that relationship. Struggling for funds and some measure of long-term stability, and therefore feeling themselves already harassed by a multitude of real or imagined, direct or indirect political pressures, public broadcasting executives will naturally not actively seek the mobilization of large groups of their audience—unless, of course, that energy can be controlled and directed according to the needs of the institution.[11]

During the mid–1970s, some very vocal and highly visible groups and individuals committed to public broadcasting's mandate, to the chagrin of both CPB and ACNO, openly challenged the Corporation's performance while others withdrew their support altogether. In 1973, the AFL–CIO, NOW, and the NAACP broke with ACNO on the issues of increased imports of foreign productions, low wages, and poor employment record for women and minorities. Led by Congressmen William Clay (D-MO) and Parren Mitchell (D-MD)—neither of whom were members of any public broadcasting subcommittees—on July 20, 1973, representatives of the National Black Media Coalition and then FCC Commissioner Benjamin Hooks testified on the House floor that the CPB had violated the Civil Rights Acts. At the 1976 CPB authorization hearings, these interest groups were joined by the National Coalition of Independent Broadcasting Producers, and all gave testimony on the CPB's failure to adhere to the diversity mandate.

Just as he had done in 1973, then House Communications and Power Subcommittee Chairman Torbert MacDonald admonished both ACNO and the CPB "to get more grassroots support."[12] By 1976, strident advocates and critics unequivocally concluded that "public involvement" in public television was a myth. Leaders of special interest groups accused the CPB of exploiting their representation of the "grassroots" public and lobby activities to secure increased funding. It was alleged that these efforts only benefitted narrow interests within the CPB bureaucracy rather than culminating in compliance to its legislative mandate—the promotion of diversity in programming and employment. The 1988 hearings found even more members of minority groups and independent producers pleading with Congress to mandate CPB compliance with the diversity clause and to stipulate a line-item allocation to independent producers.[13]

Some senior officers and members of the public broadcasting industry also maintained that the organization of public television was inadequate. The view expressed by former PBS President Larry Grossman was not uncommon.

What's wrong is that the system, the structure of public broadcasting as it has been designed in this country is so diffuse, duplicative, bureaucratic, confusing, frustrating, and senseless that it is a miracle [it has] survived at all.

It is a system no one in the outside world understands or can penetrate. It is a system that keeps public broadcasting at war with itself. It is a system that insures that public television will remain mired in second class status, with a top heavy, expensive, and stifling bureaucracy; a handicap in attracting or retaining truly creative and talented people, and an incapacity to make timely program decisions.[14]

SUMMARY

Why did formerly staunch supporters become such ardent critics of public television? The discussion thus far and organization theory suggest that public broadcasting's situation of resource dependence determined both the organization and performance of a national system of public television. As groups coalesced to build support for the enactment and subsequently to secure stable funding for the continued operation of public television, in the presence of diverse and disparate goals for the enterprise, they also competed over the policy's priorities and the distribution of benefits. The resource dependence model also suggests that over the years, some coalition members wielded greater influence over public television's fates and fortunes than others. Clearly, the telecommunications industry, educational broadcasters, and private philanthropy exercised more discretion over the definition of means and ends than the public, membership groups, and the audience.

Even today, before one accepts the criticisms and allegations frequently hurled at public broadcasting—as self-serving and ineffective—at their face value, one must understand the politics of the market managers of this public organization confront as they maneuver through the budgetary process. More than any other factor, the dependence upon

Congress and the executive, as dominant coalition partners providing the critical yet scarce resources, constrains the effectiveness of public television. Not only do these coalition members define the public organization's mandate and terms of compliance, they also define and provide the means by which goals are met.

Because Congress and the executive recognize the need to define policies broadly enough to encompass all publics, more often than not public organizations are given mandates that are intentionally vague and ill-defined. Broadly defined policies designed to appeal to multiple publics experience less opposition to passage than narrowly and well-defined ones. Therefore, the mandates of the 1967 Public Broadcasting and the 1934 Communications Acts, "to encourage the growth and development of noncommercial educational radio and television broadcasting" and "serve the public interest, convenience, and necessity," are difficult to achieve or evaluate. When one reads the Congressional Declaration of Policy for the 1967 Act and its amendments, one is more apt to conclude that public television is a panacea rather than conclude it is a pork barrel.

NOTES

1. The source of this broadcast function rests in the notion that the airwaves are socially owned or "public" rights given away as franchises granted by the FCC to private companies, television and radio licensees. In return for the allocation of an invaluable broadcast frequency, the licensee is expected to broadcast programs that serve the public interest, convenience, and necessity.

2. For transmission beyond 187–500 kilocycles, a licensee was required to specify frequency and broadcast hours and be supervised by a federally licensed operator (Blakeley, 1979, p. 35).

3. In 1912, there were 1,224 amateur licensees as compared to 405 ship-station and 123 land-station licensees. By 1923, the total number of radio licenses was reduced to 576, which were held by telecommunications manufacturers (39 percent), educational institutions (12 percent), publishers (12 percent), department stores (5 percent), and religious institutions (2 percent). Local governments, automobile dealers, theater owners, and banks accounted for the balance (30 percent). See Robert Blakeley, To Serve the Public Interest (Syracuse, NY: Syracuse University Press, 1979), p. 35.

4. Interconnection is a most critical and efficient operation in broadcasting as it permits the simultaneous transmission of a single program over multiple stations. In its absence, a single program must be duplicated and then distributed to each and every station that chooses to air it before it is broadcast. This causes queuing and inventory problems for stations, particularly noncommercial ones with far smaller budgets than commercial stations and networks.

5. Membership in the NAEB included Richard B. Hull, Harold B. McCarthy, George Probst, Wilbur Schramm, and Robert Hudson—all associated with major

universities in the United States and each a distinguished pioneer in radio broadcasting. See Blakeley (1979) for a more detailed account.

6. Financial support has also been provided by the Sloan, J. C. Penney, and Payne foundations. From 1951 to 1977, the Ford Foundation contributed $289 million to public television, of which $170 million has been committed since the establishment of CPB. Even the networks have made substantial contributions, with CBS topping the list in 1968 with a grant of $1 million.

7. Network Project, *The Fourth Network* (New York: Columbia University Press, 1971), p. 5; and Smith, 1973.

8. See Network Project, 1971, p. 7; and Blakeley, 1979.

9. See Donald L. Guimary, *Citizens Groups and Broadcasting* (New York: Praeger, 1975), p. 31.

10. Interview, respondent #9, 10/10/84. Also see Blakeley, 1979, p. 225; and Willard D. Rowland in Douglas Cater and Michael Nyan (Eds.), *The Future of Public Broadcasting* (New York: Praeger, 1976).

11. Rowland, 1976, pp. 113–114. Also see Smith, 1973, and Blakeley, 1979.

12. Marquis, 1979, p. 13. Also see Smith, 1973, and Rowland, 1976.

13. Congressional Hearings Documents: Office of Education, Special Institutions, and Related Agencies Appropriations, House, October 1987; Senate November, 1987; March, 1988.

14. Larry Grossman's remarks are taken from the official statement by Frederick Wiseman submitted to the Senate Communications Sub-Committee, Committee on Science, Commerce and Transportation, March 15, 1988.

3

The Organization of Public Broadcasting

In order to conclusively rule out the pork barrel allegation in favor of panacea or to further speculate whether tax dollars should be used to fund the public television industry, first, it is necessary to describe the organization of public broadcasting. Although public broadcasting has operated under six administrations, Presidents Johnson, Nixon, Carter, and Reagan have exercised more profound influence over its organization. These presidents imposed decision hierarchies that not only defined the organization of public broadcasting, but also determined the budgetary and policy outcomes of public television over time. Executive turnover, competition over goals and benefits among coalition partners, and the grossly underestimated costs of the enterprise resulted in the repeated reorganization of public broadcasting. Each administration's modifications of public broadcasting's organizational structure gave rise to political, strategic, and budgetary outcomes that radically altered public television effectiveness.

In this chapter, the recurrent modifications of public broadcasting's organizational structure are examined. The chapter begins with the enactment of public broadcasting policy as a government-sponsored enterprise and a description of the organizational environment of public television. The entities charged with oversight and implementation of the national systems of public telecommunications are identified. In this chapter, the budgetary and decision-making hierarchies established under the Johnson, Nixon, and Carter presidencies are delineated. Theoretical integration for these analyses is provided by the rational and resource dependence models.

THE JOHNSON ADMINISTRATION

The Road to Expeditious Passage

Members of the 1966 Carnegie Commission defined the goal of public television: to improve and expand noncommercial communication services for the public by providing insulated, stable, and increased cash flow to local stations derived directly from taxation on the sale of television sets. To accomplish this goal, the Commission proposed twelve recommendations to implement the national system of educational television.[1] The Carnegie proposals met with enthusiastic acceptance from proponents of public broadcasting. The Ford Foundation lent vigorous support. Representatives from Health, Education, and Welfare and the National Association of Educational Broadcasters met with presidential advisor C. Douglas Cater, and enlisted his support. Cater then took the lead in developing public and legislative consensus; even President Lyndon Johnson endorsed the Carnegie proposals. Despite their rationality, the recommendations were not adopted as proposed.

Timely passage of a public broadcasting act required some modification of the Carnegie proposals by a then amicable White House in anticipation of opposition from the House Ways and Means Committee, commercial broadcasters, and television set manufacturers. In lieu of an excise tax on the sale of TV sets, President Johnson suggested that operating support for public broadcasting be provided by congressional appropriations funneled through the Department of Health, Education, and Welfare. Provisions for the development of a nationwide system of public radio, service to under- and unserved audiences, equal employment opportunity, and minority employment were also added to this legislation. More importantly, the provision for long-range financing was deleted, given the budgetary constraints caused by the Vietnam War.

On March 5, 1967, Senator Warren Magnuson (D-WA) introduced a bill that implemented President Johnson's priorities and the modified Carnegie Commission recommendations. This bill had substantial backing from the commercial networks—including a pledge from CBS for $1 million to the CPB. The networks expected public television to provide a service that they could not provide profitably—quality arts and information programming.

Opposition to the bill was limited and low-key. The only opposition came from a few Republicans and southern Democrats who feared that such an agency would produce federally controlled telecasts or become a propaganda channel for the incumbent administration (Blakeley, 1979, p. 172). Fred Friendly, originator of the 1966 Ford Foundation proposal to operate communications satellites, presented the only objections to the funding mechanism. He believed that financial support for public affairs and news programming must come from sources other than Congressional appropriations as discretionary insulation might be sacrificed (ibid.).

The 1967 Public Broadcasting Act

Public Law 90–129, the Public Broadcasting Act of 1967, established the CPB as a government-sponsored enterprise and made it less vulnerable to the complexities of the budgetary process.[2] The CPB was established, financed, and monitored as an account within HEW under the Office of Education (OE). Through his legislative influence, President Johnson gave public broadcasting direct access to the budgetary process by allowing the CPB to make its budget submissions directly to Congress. As a HEW-related agency, potential opposition to the public broadcasting bill was minimized. By funneling financing through the OE rather than seeking autonomous long-term financing as an independent agency, the CPB had no separate Treasury account. Instead, the OE was the conduit for CPB funding and oversight.

This Act also called for the formation of a fifteen-member Board of Directors appointed by the president with the advice and consent of the Senate to implement and oversee the administration of a national system of public broadcasting. Of the appointed members, only eight could share the same political party affiliation as the president. The CPB board was expressly forbidden from involvement in any political activity and its composition was mandated to be as culturally, professionally, and regionally diverse as the American society.

The CPB was authorized to create two entities to interconnect the stations, distribute programs, and provide other services that enhanced the national and local programming mission. The Public Broadcasting Service (PBS) was charted for television in 1969 and National Public Radio (NPR) was chartered in 1970.[3]

Organizational Structure: 1967–1972

Under the 1967 Act, Corporation for Public Broadcasting policy making fell within several jurisdictions: four congressional committees, two bureaus, two agencies, and a commission. The Senate Communications Subcommittee, the House Interstate and Foreign Commerce Committee, and the House and Senate Appropriations Subcommittees for Labor–HEW and Related Agencies conducted authorizing and appropriations hearings for the CPB itself. Having no separate Treasury account, these funds were disbursed and accounted for by HEW's Office of Education. Additional program production funds were granted for instructional programming as a line-item allocation from the Office of Education and for cultural-informational programming from the National Endowment for the Humanities. Funds for public broadcasting facilities—equipment, construction, maintenance, and expansion but, exclusive of land and buildings—were provided under a separate program, the Public Telecommunications Facilities Program (PTFP). These funds were funneled from appropriations to the National Telecommunications and Information Administration (NTIA) directly to local stations as technical improvement grants.[4]

In short, three federal agencies were charged with distributive discretion and oversight for public broadcasting: NTIA, HEW–OE, and CPB. Policy oversight and guidance of public broadcasting, as in commercial broadcasting, were exercised by the FCC in its role as guardian of the airwaves. The National Endowment for the Humanities only distributed funds as project grants to various public broadcasting entities. Subordinate production and operation functions were delegated to the national audio and video entities, National Public Radio and the Public Broadcasting Service. Direct delivery of public broadcasting services was provided by the local stations.

At the lower level of organization, special interest groups were indirectly incorporated into the structure of public broadcasting. Local station managers worked with PBS and NPR largely to express their needs and preferences for interconnection, programming, and facilities improvement. Programming was produced by regional production centers and local studios, then shared with local stations throughout the system. In addition, a representative organization of station managers, the National Association of Pubic Television Stations (NAPTS, which changed its name to the Association for Public Broadcasting in 1988) lobbied for public television station interests in congressional hearings and meetings with agency officials.[5] However, station managers had minimal direct input into the determination of federal allocations to the local stations.

Similarly, independent producers collaborated with PBS, NPR, and CPB largely to bid or compete for program production grants. Other special interests were formally folded into public broadcasting as an Advisory Council of National Organizations (ACNO), which advised the CPB Board of Directors.[6] Thus, access to the public broadcasting policy process by more "marginal" coalition partners and the public was proxied primarily through and at the direction of the Corporation for Public Broadcasting.

Corporation control for the overall operation of the system, including local station programming, reached its apex under President Johnson's Administration. The CPB was staffed by a substantial number of professionals with proven track records in educational broadcasting and directed by a strong board. Under Frank Pace, the CPB's first chairman of the board, and John Macy, its first president, CPB operation was

Figure 3.1
Public Broadcasting Decision Hierarchy: 1972

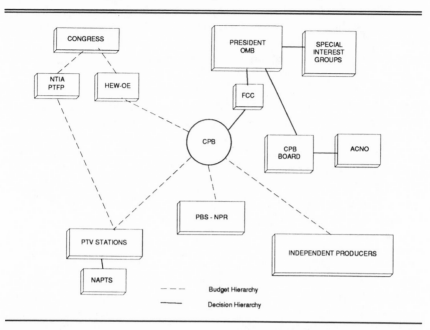

highly centralized.[7] In these early years, public television enjoyed direct linkage to the budgetary process and experienced considerable discretionary autonomy and growth. Figure 3.1 depicts these relationships. It also reveals, with great clarity, public television's absolute vulnerability and dependence upon an array of government decision makers for essential monetary and linking resources.

THE NIXON ADMINISTRATION

Pressures for Restructuring Public Broadcasting

Administrative turnover brought public broadcasting's growth and success to a screeching halt. A heretofore highly supportive environment was, in very short order, transformed into an adversarial one during President Richard Nixon's Administration. Although the reasons for this transformation are many, three are especially important. In addition to executive and agency differences over preferences for public television policy itself, the tension between local station managers and CPB officials over centralized control as well as the grossly underestimated costs of a national system of public broadcasting led to the total overhaul of the Corporation and its entities in 1973.

The unexpected costs of a greatly expanded national system of public television stations played a catalytic role in the reorganization of public broadcasting. Initially, Congress expected to set up public broadcasting and then withdraw federal support as the CPB became self-sustaining. However, the federal government's commitment to develop and maintain a system of public broadcasting required significantly higher fixed costs commitments than its planners had envisioned. The rapid growth and development of a public television industry through the proliferation of newly licensed local stations greatly outpaced the resources appropriated to it. The number of local stations nearly doubled from 126 PTV stations in 1967 to 233 in 1972. The subsequent increased demand from local stations for more funds and discretion exceeded the capacity of the CPB to provide the necessary resources.

Furthermore, public television's legal, budgetary, and discretionary fragmentation prompted persistent coordination and control problems between agency officials and local station managers. Conflict over a highly centralized nationally controlled organization versus a highly localized one was fueled by the decision-making and budgetary hierarchies of public broadcasting itself. For example, in 1971, local stations vied openly with the CPB and PBS for more influence in allocative and programming discretion, while the CPB and PBS were embroiled in conflict with the White House over controversial programming. Local public television stations formed regional alliances that simultaneously lobbied Congress and the White House for the increased and direct allocation of funds with broader spending criteria.

Structural Overhaul. Under President Nixon, additional layers of bureaucracy were imposed to monitor public broadcasting operations and discretion by enhancing the jurisdiction of the Executive Office of the President (EOP). The Office of Telecommunications Policy (OTP) was established to manage the broadcast spectrum and provide direct oversight of the facilities program (PTFP) and national telecommunications policy in 1970. By 1971, the OTP had become so heavily involved in public television policy that its General Council, Antonin Scalia, drafted a long-term financing bill "which would have increased and guaranteed CPB funds to stations, given HEW authority for non-broadcast and ITV activities, and [provided] $93 million for FY 1973, and $100 million annually thereafter through FY 1977" (Marquis, 1979, p. 13). At the direction of H. R. Haldeman, then White House Chief of Staff, the EOP also directly shaped public television policy. The EOP made future funding contingent upon public television reorganization. Under pressure from highly publicized and persistent threats to terminate the Corporation's very existence as well as the 1973 appropriations veto, CPB officers capitulated and restructured public television.

Lastly, the policy shift that accompanied executive turnover also transformed the organization of public broadcasting. The White House staff's characterization of public television as "antiadministration" culminated in the budget-imposed reorganization of public broadcasting (ibid.). Not only did the airing of news and public affairs programs critical of the Nixon Administration diminish executive support for the agency, it raised the ire of White House staff who mounted a campaign against public television and its officials.

Justified on the basis of the "new federalism," public television reorganization was consistent with Nixon's popular mandate "to put money where the needs are. . . . And the power to spend it where the people are."[8] The delegation of discretionary and enhanced budgetary autonomy to the managers of local public television stations, as the proxies for local publics, was simultaneously a step toward this new federalism, a step toward the increased accountability of public broadcasting, and a step further away from long-term politically insulated financing. Although White House intervention in CPB policy and the presidential veto of the FY 1973 CPB appropriation bill forced a highly political and controversial compromise that led to the resignations of CPB President John Macy and his top aides, more importantly, these executive-level actions redefined the CPB–PBS relationship, role, and responsibilities.

In order to secure long-term funding and regain presidential support, the Corporation for Public Broadcasting and the Public Broadcasting Service negotiated the landmark "partnership agreement." This agreement revamped CPB–PBS programming operations in three strategic areas: interconnection, discretion, and distribution. Specifically, the partnership agreement:

1. Provided that PBS would continue to operate the interconnection on behalf of its member stations under the direction of its station-controlled board. CPB would finance only technical operations through a contract with PBS, and would leave to PBS's station members the financing of such activities as programming, promotion, public information, research, and representation.
2. Established a significant increase in CPB's discretionary funds—Community Service Grants—to stations. These unrestricted grants to television stations were to rise to 50 percent of the CPB appropriation once it reached $80 million. The consequence of increasing the amount CPB "passed through" to stations was to reduce the amount of money and discretion that CPB itself had for programming.
3. Altered the programming–funding process employed by CPB and PBS. While CPB was permitted to make all final decisions about programs financed through its TV activities department, the staff was instructed to consult on program decision with the staff at PBS.[9]

These provisions gave increased financing, autonomy, and discretion to local public television stations while the Corporation for Public Broadcasting gained increased and stable funding at the expense of diminished centralized control. President Nixon's "signing of the CPB authorization indicated that the Chief Executive had been at least partially appeased by the CPB–PBS partnership now in effect."[10] As White House Assistant Secretary Gerald Warren surmised, the bill signed by Nixon on August 6, 1973, furthered the "goal of achieving this principle of localism, and represents the administration's continued support."[11]

Organizational Structure: 1974–1978

The Nixon Administration's reorganization of public television substantially altered CPB discretion, autonomy, and performance by modifying public broadcasting's interdependence relations at all levels of organization. Three strategies were used to make these adjustments and, thereby, alter interdependencies at the boundaries: board appointments, enhanced bureaucratization, and the delegation of discretion and autonomy to local station managers at the expense of agency officials. For example, of the fifteen Johnson CPB board appointments, only four were reappointed. Nixon appointed ten, allegedly highly partisan, board members during his two-year tenure in office. Citing White House interference, then CPB chairman Frank Pace declined renomination. This newly constituted board negotiated the CPB–PBS Partnership Agreement in order to restore funding frozen by the veto.

The greatly enlarged role of the OTP, the Nixon veto, and the subsequent partnership agreement enhanced bureaucratization and decreased discretion and autonomy for both the CPB and PBS. From 1974 onward, the CPB would be viewed as a mere administrative apparatus, a pipeline for funneling tax dollars to the public broadcasting industry. Under pressure from OTP and at the direction of a more highly politicized Board of Directors, the Corporation removed from PBS certain legal, research, public awareness, and programming functions—particularly, the ultimate decision making for program production grants, support, and acquisition. Through the revised partnership agreement, PBS continued to operate the interconnection on behalf of its member stations under the direction of a now station-controlled board of directors. With the establishment of the Station Program Cooperative (SPC) in 1974, PBS became the agent for local stations by coordinating the program selection and acquisition process.

Consequently, the CPB financed only technical operations through a contract with PBS, and left programming activities to PBS station members. Although the partnership agreement brought significantly increased funding for public television, most of these funds were passed directly through to the local stations in the form of unrestricted grants—

Figure 3.2
Public Broadcasting Decision Hierarchy: 1974

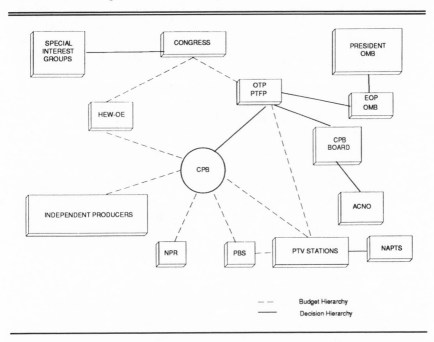

community service grants (CSGs). Needless to say, the receipt of unrestricted grants, essentially money to "be used at the discretion of the recipient for purposes related primarily to the production or acquisition of programming," afforded greater autonomy for local public television stations.[12] Figure 3.2 illustrates these new interdependence relationships.

THE CARTER ADMINISTRATION

Bureaucratic Retrenchment

The administration of President Jimmy Carter proved to be a much more favorable environment for public television than its predecessor. Neither threatened by budgetary cutback nor veto, the growth of public broadcasting remained stable and expansionary from 1976 until 1982. The organization of public broadcasting was also least complex during this period. With his mandate to eliminate government waste and the inappropriateness of HEW's Office of Education rules for CPB spending oversight, President Carter scaled down the public broadcasting bureaucracy.

Under the Carter Administration, the CPB appropriation was removed from Labor–HEW and Related Agencies jurisdiction and transferred to the House Committee on Communications Subcommittee on Telecommunications, Consumer Protection, and Finance. A separate Trust Fund was established with the Treasury to simplify the accounting procedure. This allowed funds to be passed directly from the Treasury to the CPB. Equally important, the Office of Telecommunications Policy was eliminated and the facilities program, PTFP, was returned to NTIA jurisdiction. The reduced bureaucratization and increased autonomy secured the Corporation's position as a government-sponsored enterprise.

Congress returned to more direct oversight of public broadcasting by providing appropriations to the telecommunications entities themselves, NTIA and CPB. Both the National Telecommunications and Information Administration and the Corporation for Public broadcasting passed even more funds through to the local stations directly. The NTIA expanded public broadcasting coverage by awarding increased technology grants to more licensees. The CPB awarded larger community service grants to the local stations. The Corporation also continued allocations to the Public Broadcasting Service for interconnection and program distribution. Local stations coordinated the activities of program production through the regional production centers and program acquisition through PBS.

Under President Carter, the public broadcasting budget rose and the organizational modifications to the Corporation reinforced implementation of the diversity goals of public broadcasting. Both CPB board appointments and internal budget allocations promoted minority and female involvement in public television. Of his seven new board appointees, two were women and two were minority males (African American and Hispanic). Carter also retained two female Republicans initially appointed by President Ford. Moreover, increased appropriations earmarked more funding to independent producers and minority and female recruitment, hiring, and training.

Boundary modifications implemented by the Carter Administration have remained unaltered, and provide the present structure of public broadcasting organization. Figure 3.3 depicts these boundary modifications.

THE REAGAN ADMINISTRATION

During President Reagan's Administration, no alterations were made to public broadcasting's organizational structure, however, changes to the Corporation for Public Broadcasting's Board of Directors were substantive. CPB board bylaws were statutorily modified. The fifteen-member Board of Directors was reduced to ten, with a maximum of six to be appointed from the same political party as the President. This scaled-down board now included local station representation that had been

Figure 3.3
Public Broadcasting Decision Hierarchy: 1978

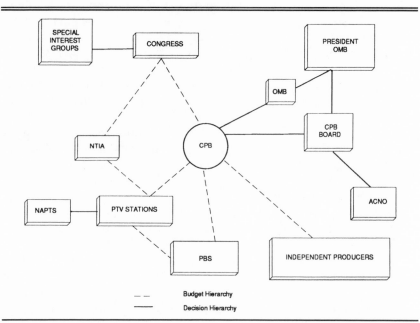

prohibited under prior administrations. Two seats, one for television and one for radio, were reserved for licensees. Consistent with his appointments in other areas of the federal government, Reagan made highly partisan appointments to the CPB Board of Directors in return for campaign support. As a result, the Corporation, once again, underwent extreme politicization.

For example, former board Chairperson Sharon Rockefeller was unseated by Sonia Landau, the former head of Women for Reagan–Bush. Four other leaders of the Reagan–Bush election campaign were also appointed to the CPB board to replace Democrats whose terms had expired. In addition, President Reagan's appointees pressed for consistency and adherence to the "Administration's line" in their board actions.[13]

In 1985, the CPB board took one action that was quite consistent with the Administration's line that viewed Russia as "the evil empire." Controversy over the CPB program exchange trip to Moscow climaxed with the resignation of President Ed Pfister. This trip had been proposed and approved during Rockefeller's term as chairman. However, the board later voted, by a margin of 6–4, to cancel the Corporation's role in the trip after Landau assumed chairmanship. Landau maintained the "CPB is a custodian of federal money. . . . [We are] opposed to the use of federal money for this activity . . . it is not the Corporation's role to negotiate with foreign governments or any government with state-controlled television. . . . [This is a] USIA and Department of State area."[14] CPB President Ed Pfister responded, "This is a private entity, as such federal dollars become private dollars. . . . Public Broadcasting has a history of dealing with the U.S.S.R." Board member William Hanley, a new Reagan appointee, then added, "Private versus public is not the issue but, will CPB involvement hurt future CPB authorizations and appropriations? Further, the board should consider the extent of CPB participation in activities of this sort regardless of the destination."[15]

Under Landau's leadership, the board also amended sections of its own bylaws in order to render Corporation officials more accountable. For example, the General Counsel, Program Fund Director, and Congressional Liaison were made directly accountable to the CPB board and the CPB management, instead of the CPB management exclusively. Thereby, these officers' discretion became even less insulated from executive oversight as proxied by the Board of Directors. The board also instructed the General Counsel "to be present at all CPB board meetings, including executive sessions, except at the option of the board."[16] Section 4.11 of the CPB bylaws was amended to read:

General Counsel is the chief legal officer of the Corporation and provides advice and counsel to the Board of Directors and Management of the Corporation on legal, public policy, legislative, and regulatory matters affecting public broadcasting and the operation of the Corporation. The General Counsel is responsible for, and generally oversees, the conduct of the Corporation's legal affairs, including the retention of outside counsel where appropriate and necessary, and provides representation and legal support services required for day-to-day corporate operations.[17]

THEORETICAL INTEGRATION

Expediency Begets Nonrational Organization

When one applies organization theory to public broadcasting, two generalizations can be made and extended to public organizations. First, organization of the Corporation for Public Broadcasting was nonrational. Second, the Corporation is adaptive. For the Corporation—and public organizations generally—the conditions of the rational model are never fulfilled. The Corporation for Public Broadcasting was not established as an entity with internally well-defined goals and means nor clear and centralized lines of authority on efficiency grounds—a pyramidal decision hierarchy to ensure minimal costs and maximal gains. Instead, public broadcasting is a typical example of organized anarchy—the nonrational organization of public policy.[18]

Dependent upon the convergence of diverse issues, interests, means and goals, the strategy pursued by President Johnson to assure passage of the Public Broadcasting Act deemphasized differences. It was a strategy that maximized enactment by minimizing opposition. A mission statement was defined that embraced all relevant constituencies and a funding apparatus was devised that did not antagonize the communications industry. The outcome was a highly fragmented, but federally funded organization constituted by disparate and competing interests.

Dependent upon the appropriations process, the Corporation for Public Broadcasting is most responsive to executive and congressional preferences. The repeated restructuring of the Corporation demonstrates how partisan politics and the competing interests of coalition partners constrain organizational effectiveness. As a coalition dependent upon politicians and other special interest groups, the Corporation's mission and structure are defined by a dynamic, if not volatile, environment. The Corporation is adaptive—as are other public organizations—because organizational survival is the paramount goal. The Corporation is most adaptive to the demands of the executive and Congress because these coalition members control the appropriations process. As enacted, the Corporation cannot survive without increased and stable appropriations.

Given the public organization's need for increased and stable appropriations, the resource dependence model suggests the management of interdependence relations—ties of mutual dependence between the public organization, Congress, and the executive. These ties can be manipulated in order to minimize the loss of discretion and autonomy, reduce dominance by a particular actor(s), and stabilize the resource exchange. Hence, the organization tries to incorporate the resources within itself through structural or relational modifications of its interdependence.

Managers of public organizations are greatly restricted in their choice of strategies to modify the ties of mutual dependence. Because laws limit these managers both in the choice of whether they may seek alternative suppliers of essential resources as well as the manner and methods they may use, generally, only two types of interdependence manipulation are possible in the public organization. Both are variations on the coalition formation strategy. Managers of the public organization can exercise exclusive dependence on one or more actors—namely, Congress and the executive—adhere to their expectations, then request only modest increments in their budget appropriations. Or, when the legal mandate so stipulates, managers of the public organization can develop alternative sources of resource supply through the management of interdependence with multiple resource suppliers and compliance to the consequent tasks demands—including those of Congress and the executive.[19]

Since enactment, managers of the Corporation for Public Broadcasting have modified its ties of mutual dependence. They have altered its purposes and domains—through repeated reorganization—in order to regulate and stabilize resource flows. For example, managers of the Corporation have refined and developed new staff roles in accordance with appropriations decision makers. These include redefinition of the General Counsel's duties in the CPB Board By-Laws and staff expansion in the CPB's Office of Congressional Liaison.

Managers of the Corporation also manipulate interdependence relations by maintaining constituency satisfaction and accommodating new interests. Public broadcasting staff work with congressional and executive staff to formulate mutually acceptable appropriations bills.[20] Corporation officials also strive to keep coalition partners on board by adjusting to their performance demands in accordance with the resources they supply. For example, Corporation officials increasingly seek and consolidate support from public television stations. Corporation staff also rally and coordinate representatives from public broadcasting special interest groups to provide testimony at congressional hearings. In short, Corporation for Public Broadcasting management successfully adapts to the exigencies of a dynamic environment—executive turnover and structural complexity—and, thereby, assures organizational survival.

SUMMARY

Throughout its short history, the organization of public broadcasting has undergone repeated structural metamorphoses. In particular, modifications to the decision-making and budgetary hierarchies by the Johnson, Nixon, and Carter Administrations have progressively shifted control over public television policy from CPB officials to local station managers. However, changes in public broadcasting policy during the Reagan Administration were accomplished mainly through increased board politicization. These alterations of public broadcasting policy were due, in large part, to the underestimated costs of this new public policy, problems of coordination and control that arise from competition among coalition partners and structural complexity, and changes in the overall political priorities and presidential preferences that ensue from executive turnover.

The Corporation for Public Broadcasting represented a new commitment to a new constituency for a new technology administered by a new organization embedded in an unstable, unpredictable, and competitive external environment with other public organizations. Managers of the CPB leapt into a market with officers of other Great Society programs only to compete with them and the Vietnam War for already scarce revenues. The increased costs of a tremendously expanded public telecommunications system and the very propulsion of public television into an arena dominated by the commercial networks also generated unanticipated financial demand. If public television was to attract and sustain an audience, it had to compete technologically and qualitatively with the commercial networks, which had, by comparison, a limitless source of financing.

When one looks at public television organization under the Johnson, Nixon, and Carter Administrations, one also recognizes that CPB and PBS reorganization ensued more from presidential policy shifts than from structural complexity or monetary costs. The seemingly never-ending reorganization of the national system of public broadcasting mirrors important partisan changes in presidential preferences for national public broadcasting policy over time. The Corporation's budget-induced capitulation to executive preferences, as dramatized by the landmark Partnership Agreement, demonstrates the role executive turnover plays in public policy implementation.

Executive turnover, more than any other factor, substantially transformed the power relations (interdependencies) within the national system of public television by progressively decentralizing discretion and increasing autonomy for local stations. Control over public television organization and policy was delegated in a direction consistent with the "new federalism." Increasingly, control was shifted from agency administrators at the national level to station managers at the local level largely by politicizing the Corporation for Public Broadcasting's budgetary process.

NOTES

1. See Appendix for the twelve recommendations.

2. As a government-sponsored enterprise, the budgetary process is abridged. The CPB makes its formal budget submission directly to Congress. In order to maintain amicable relations with the OMB, however, the CPB budget officer informally apprises the OMB examiner of the year's request figures. Usually, the CPB request is much larger than the OMB marks. If there is a significant discrepancy between the position developed by OMB in accordance with the President' priorities and preferences, then the OMB requests a budget hearing. When this occurs, the CPB budget officer goes over to OMB and presents justification for the CPB budget request. Over the years, the CPB has received only one written pass-back from OMB. The CPB is not held to the formality of a final appeal. (Interview: #17, 4/85.)

3. Although the NPR also serves as an interesting case for study, only public television is the subject of this analysis. Therefore, no further mention will be made of the radio broadcasting mission of the CPB.

4. The NTIA is the principal executive branch adviser to the President on domestic and international communications policy. It manages the federal government's use of the broadcast spectrum, the emergency use and planning of

the military spectrum, and performs extensive research in telecommunications sciences.

5. In 1991, America's Public Television Stations, Inc., was recognized by the District of Columbia as a 504 C–4, a representation group of its parent organization, the Association for Public Broadcasting (formerly known as the National Association for Public Television Stations).

6. Initially, ACNO was a membership organization that represented twenty-six national groups selected by the CPB board to provide advocacy and advice. These included the National PTA, AFL–CIO, NAACP, National Organization of Women, National Education Association, American Bar Association, and the United Jaycees.

7. The CPB board is reputed to have never been as diverse as its mandate authorized; frequently, it is cited as heavily biased in favor of the sitting administration. See the Network Project, 1971, and Cater et al., *The Future of Public Broadcasting*, 1976.

8. See *Presidential Documents*, January 1–April 4, 1974, p. 42.

9. Carnegie Commission, pp. 45–46.

10. *Broadcasting*, August 13, 1973, p. 23.

11. Ibid.

12. Corporation of Public Broadcasting, CSG Distribution Criteria, p. 38.

13. CPB Board Notes, 6/27/85.

14. Ibid.

15. Ibid.

16. Ibid.

17. By-Laws, Corporation for Public Broadcasting, 1985, Sect. 4.11.

18. See James G. March and Johan P. Olsen, *Ambiguity and Choice in Organizations* (Oslo, Norway: Universitesforlaget, 1979).

19. Fannie Mae, the Securities Investors Corporation, and other government-sponsored enterprises, which operate outside the established legal system, are such examples. According to Harold Seidman (1988), these organizations have the budgetary and discretionary autonomy to determine both the suppliers of needed resources and the terms of compliance. Most government-sponsored enterprises are free to "find the ways and the means to finance programs 'off budget' " as long as they are in accordance with presidential preferences, particularly those governed by a presidentially appointed board of directors.

20. See Malcolm Goggin, *Policy Implementation by Design* (Knoxville: University of Tennessee Press, 1987).

4

The Politics of Public Television and the Search for Survival

Executive turnover has transformed the organization of public television and heralded atypical budget growth. This transformation has affected public broadcasting policy and public television performance. Increased board politicization and threats of severe budgetary cutback have modified public broadcasting organization and performance since its inception. Progressively, the executive and Congress have relieved the CPB of its discretionary autonomy in favor of politically prudent allocations to special interest groups directly from Congress. In this chapter, the politics that generated these outcomes are described and examined. Public broadcasting's dependence upon coalition partners, who provide resources critical to organizational survival, is shown to alter strategic behavior and performance markedly.

More than any other factor, the strategic behavior of public television is determined by survival goals. Decision making in the Corporation for Public Broadcasting is constrained significantly by the need to comply with the expectations of powerful political actors—the executive and Congress as dominant coalition partners, who authorize and appropriate critical financing. In its search for survival, the Corporation's organizational effectiveness is determined by its ability to secure increased appropriations, not strategic management. In short, public television's autonomy, discretion, and goal attainment are limited more by its dependence upon political market forces than economic ones.

In this chapter, the legislative and appropriations history of the Corporation for Public Broadcasting is analyzed. Herein it is demonstrated that public television has indeed been more responsive to the dynamic demands of the coalition's dominant members—the executive, Congress, and local stations—than to its more marginal members. From this analysis of public broadcasting legislation, three phases of public television transformation are distinguished: Johnson, Nixon–Ford, and Carter–Reagan. Under these Chief Executives, budget outcomes and decision hierarchies were imposed as legislative mandates that substantially altered public television's strategic behavior and organizational effectiveness.

In addition to demands for compliance from the dominant coalition partners, public broadcasting is pressured by the special interest groups that coalesce to enact an environment for public television. At each phase, special interest groups within the public television industry lobby Congress for increased control over the system, diversity in both employment and programming, and a larger role in program production. These issues are important to local station managers, educational broadcasters, independent producers, and other noncommercial broadcasting professionals as well as minorities and women. From agency officials with a national vision for public television to professionals and technicians seeking a market for their products, all demand direct benefits from public broadcasting legislation. Members of these special interests groups, who once concertedly lobbied for federal financing of public television, now compete over the spoils from this public organization.

Chronologically, Phase I gives a description of the performance and politics of public television introduced by Public Law 90–129 from its inception in 1967 until 1972—the Johnson legacy. Phase II presents a description of the performance and politics from 1972 until 1976, the Nixon–Ford years.[1] Public Laws 92–411 and 94–192 are most important during this phase. Lastly, Phase III provides a description of the performance and politics of public television from 1976 through 1988, the Carter– Reagan years. The enactment of Public laws 95–567, 97–35, and 100–626 are noteworthy because they profoundly altered Corporation budget and policy outcomes during Phase III. The analysis of each phase takes into account the lag effect of the forward funding provision and administrative overlap. The correspondence between the legislative, budgetary, and administrative history of public broadcasting is illustrated in Table 4.1.

PHASE I: THE JOHNSON LEGACY

Under the leadership of President Lyndon Johnson, the Corporation for Public Broadcasting was legally mandated as a private, nonprofit government organization by the Public Broadcasting Act of 1967, PL 90–129. This Act sought to service a segment of society whose needs were hitherto unfulfilled by government or private business. The CPB mission was to provide a dependable vehicle for high-quality and diverse cultural and informational programming on a continuous basis through the use

Table 4.1
Legislative History

Phase I		Phase II		Phase III	
Johnson		Nixon		Carter	
Pub. Broad Act (PL 90-129)	1967	Veto & PL92-411 (Con. Res)			1981
	1968		1973	1978 Financing Act (PL 95-567)	1982
		(PL 93-84)	1974		1983
	1970				
(PL 91-437)	1971				
	1972				
		Ford		Reagan	
			1975		
			1976	1981 Omnibus Act	1984
		1975 Financing Act (PL 94-192)	1977	(PL 97-35)	1985
			1978	(PL 98-214)	1986
			1979		
			1980		1987
				(PL 99-272)	1988
					1989
					1990
					1991
				(PL 100-626)	1992
					1993

of radio and television. From 1967 until 1972, public television experienced a period of phenomenal growth and programming success. While the number of public television stations increased, from 153 to 220, program production also reached its zenith.

After protracted negotiations, the Public Broadcasting Service was chartered by the Corporation in 1969. As the programming apparatus or "network" for the national system of public television, the mission of the Public Broadcasting Service (PBS) was to provide interconnection management and operation for local public television stations. Under President Johnson, PBS was administered mainly by noncommercial broadcasters. PBS was largely composed of station members, that is, public television licensees, although several CPB senior staff and public television production staff served as general members. PBS provided highly centralized coordination of the national system of public television. Although prohibited from a direct program production function, PBS helped coordinate producers on the planning, funding, scheduling, and distribution of national programming for public television. PBS made production grants to producers to finance news, information, and entertainment programs that were subsequently distributed to local stations. PBS also developed a national schedule that was broadcast during prime and nonprime time.

During the Johnson era, several significant achievements and innovations were made by PBS. Public television's prime time audience share and popular support were increased substantially by the broadcast of cultural, educational, and scientific programs. *The Great American Dream Machine, Masterpiece Theatre, Dance in America,* and *Sesame Street* were developed during this period. Public television's programming diversity mission was fulfilled by providing national and local programming geared to previously "underserved and unserved" audiences. Programs of special interest to minorities, for example, *Soul, Black Journal,* later *Realidades, Interface,* and *Villa Allegre,* were produced and aired. Programs for audience segments previously ignored by commercial broadcasters were also provided: *Over Easy* for senior citizens, *Electric Company* and *Zoom* for children, *Nova* for the science-minded, and *Soundstage* for culture buffs. Scientific and cultural programs were produced largely through generous corporate underwriting. In fact, much of the innovative programming that public television is noted for, and much of what is continued today, was developed during Phase I.

Managers of public television took risks. Through PBS, programs were provided that contributed to the development of public television policy by presenting information and points of view absent or divergent from those of commercial broadcasting. Programs such as *Washington Week in Review, Banks and the Poor, Black Perspective on the News,* and the *McNeil–Lehrer Report* presented information to the public that the government and commercial television could not or would not. Locally, city council meetings were regularly televised. Local artists were given exposure. Educators, groups, and individuals active in community affairs were provided a forum. On the technical side, a specialized technology now widely used in commercial broadcasting was pioneered by PBS: the captioning service for the hearing impaired.

Throughout Phase I, the special interests or benefactors served by public television were many and varied. Corporate underwriters gained tax "write-offs," recognition, prestige, and influence. The broadcasting market was thrown open to new and established actors, artists, film-makers, journalists, media technicians, independent producers, edu-cators, and scientists. Less well-known broadcast journalists, such as Robert McNeil, Jim Lehrer, Bill Moyers, Sander Vanocur, and Tony Brown, became household names for news and information viewers. Prior to public television, how many Americans knew of Jacques Cousteau?

Children and adults were formally educated by public television. While three-year-olds learned reading skills via *Sesame Street*, adults earned college credit from courses aired on the college extension pro-grams. Culture-oriented viewers savored *An Evening at the Symphony* and *Theatre in America*. Minorities and women could choose from an array of programs geared to their expressed "tastes." Public television had identified and served a market that consisted of viewers who comprised the News and Information, Family Integrated Activities, Highly Diver-sified, Arts and Culture audience segments (Frank and Greenberg, 1982). Under President Johnson, public television had become an innovative educational and cultural forum that reflected the diversity of American society.

By April 1971, the Corporation for Public Broadcasting had established a successful track record with both the House and Senate Appropriations Subcommittees. The CPB had demonstrated competency in its work and leadership. Expectations, norms, and roles had developed between this public organization and the House and Senate. The CPB had gained the confidence, support, and sympathy of Congress. The supportive re-marks made by Senator Ernest Hollings (D-SC) and Representative Dan-iel Flood (D-PA) in Subcommittee hearings were typical. On April 2, 1971, Senator Hollings addressed then CPB president John W. Macy: "I am prejudiced, of course. I started the original educational TV. I ap-pointed the first PTV commission and have been a great believer in public broadcasting. I am enthused that your heading this up is going to fill a tremendous gap."[2] Similar remarks had passed from Mr. Flood to Mr. Macy during House hearings on February 26, 1971: "We are prejudiced in your favor."[3]

Consequently, the Senate and House Labor–HEW Appropriations

Subcommittees authorized the amount requested by the CPB in the 1973 Appropriations Bill, $65 million with a provision for long-term financing. This bill, PL 92–411, provided an increased appropriation of nearly 200% over that of the previous year. Passage of this bill also indicated that CPB management was effective in dispatching its policy mandate. In the eyes of the legislative branch, the CPB had, in fact, implemented programs consistent with the interests and goals of its coalition partners.

PHASE II: THE NIXON–FORD YEARS

President Richard Nixon

Much to the dismay of Congress, on June 29, 1972, President Nixon vetoed the 1973 appropriation bill. Charging that the production and distribution of controversial news and public affairs programming departed from the concept of localism, President Nixon announced that "increased and long-term funding was unwise" (PL 92–411). Differences between dominant coalition members over the priorities, expectations, and performance of public television were climaxed with a veto.

The veto created considerable upheaval for public television. Programs, particularly those news and public affairs productions critical of government performance that were judged "antiadministration" by the Nixon White House, were canceled or toned down. These included *Banks and the Poor*, *Washington Week in Review*, *Bill Moyers*, and *The Great American Dream Machine*. A poignant example of White House clandestine tinkering with public television's internal management detail is provided by the cancellation of *Banks and the Poor*. This production alleged that major banks were discriminating against the poor, many of whom were minorities, through practices of redlining. The program closed with a long, scrolling list of senators and congressmen who had (or were alleged to have) ties to the banking industry (Witherspoon and Kovitz, 1989, p. 40).

Policy-makers at CPB and PBS questioned the program's fairness. So did the White House. Enclosing a clipping about the program from the *Washington Post*, Flanigan wrote Cole asking how much money CPB had given to NET that year, and how much it had budgeted for the production center for 1971. Wrote Flanigan, "Herewith another example of NET activity that is clearly inappropriate for a government-supported organization. . . . I am directing this inquiry to you in that I think it comes better from you to the board and the management of the corporation than from the White House. Therefore, I'd appreciate you treating this inquiry in that light" (ibid.).

In a drive to admonish the general broadcast media for the alleged abuse of its role and power, through biased and irresponsible journalism,

Vice President Spiro Agnew and Office of Telecommunications Policy (OTP) Director Clay T. Whitehead undertook a two-year-long campaign of public arousal and denunciation. Their crusade ended in invocations of the Fairness Doctrine as well as the reorganization and redefinition of goals for public broadcasting.[4] Not only were commercial broadcasters threatened with FCC license revocation should they fail to "make their facilities available and grant equal time to responsible members of the community with contrasting views on various issues" but, public television also found itself mandated to promote "objectivity, fairness, and balance" in all public affairs programming.

In official statements, members of the Nixon Administration played on local public broadcasters' fears of a highly centralized "Fourth Network" and lauded the principle of "localism" in broadcasting—a buzz word for enhanced station autonomy and discretion. OTP staff stridently and publicly alleged that "public broadcasting was centralizing its forces and that the individuality of local stations was not being recognized on a national level."[5] In private, Clay T. Whitehead strove to redirect CPB funds from National Educational Television and other producers of "objectionable programs" to the local stations. In a memo, Whitehead estimated that "local station support can be bought for $30 million" (*Channels*, August 1985, p. 34).

On the morning of June 22, 1972, Clay Whitehead met with CPB consultants to reassure them of the President's intention to sign the authorization for increased CPB funding. By 4:00 P.M., in a meeting with Mr. Whitehead, FCC Chairman Dean Burch, Communications Director Herb Klein, a White House aide, and a group of thirty broadcast station executives, who controlled 110 stations, President Nixon expressed his "unhappiness over development of public TV" and questioned "the propriety of using government funds to support programming" (Dorfmann, 1973, p. 3). Given the implicit as well as explicit administration support and encouragement, local station managers openly vied with CPB and PBS for more influence in allocative decision making while the CPB and PBS were embroiled in the wrenching battle with OTP.[6]

A Revamped Public Broadcasting Service. In the wake of the Nixon veto and the administration's appeal for the media's accountability to the public, the relations between the CPB and PBS began to deteriorate. In exchange for the CPB 1973 increased budget appropriation, the Public Broadcasting Service was coerced into jettisoning an already limited programming function. PBS became a stationed-owned membership organization that enabled stations to provide and distribute programs and to determine their own broadcast schedules. With the furor from the veto and ferment from the President's men also came the resignation of CPB's first president, John Macy. Macy was replaced by former Deputy Director of the United States Information Agency, Henry Loomis, upon the recommendation of CPB Board Chairman Thomas Curtis, himself a Nixon appointee.

Organizational effectiveness was greatly constrained by congressional and administrative differences over goals, preferences, and priorities greatly constrained the Corporation for Public Broadcasting. Institutional relationships within public television were substantially transformed by the conflict between CPB and PBS over strategic behavior. Having caved in to White House pressure, CPB board members initiated three actions that precipitated a major reorganization of PBS. First, led by Loomis and Curtis, the CPB board voted to discontinue funding of all public affairs programming except *Black Journal*. Second, board members rescinded a staff commitment to provide multiyear funding to the National Public Affairs Center for Television (a division of the Greater Washington Educational Telecommunications Association, which produces news and public affairs programming for national distribution through PBS). Third, CPB board members also

unanimously voted to take from PBS certain legal, research, public awareness, and programming functions, including the decision making process, and ultimate responsibility for decisions, on program production support or acquisition (and) the pre-broadcast review of programs to determine strict adherence to objectivity and balance in all programs of a controversial nature (Carnegie Commission, 1979, p. 45).

The White House staff's perception of public broadcasting as antagonistically antiadministration resulted in the imposition of four critical constraints. These constraints undermined the very organization and function of public broadcasting by initiating both the decline of PBS and public television's shift from a forum for cultural diversity to one of cultural elitism. First, the Nixon veto led to the redefinition of the goals and means of public broadcasting, thereby restricting the CPB's strategic choice and policy-making capability. Second, limits were imposed on the capacity of public television's decision makers to render sound programmatic choices in the interests of its diverse clientele, that is, cheaper British imports in lieu of the more expensive local productions.

Third, CPB's role, influence, and power in the larger broadcasting environment were diminished. The Corporation was compelled to reduce its innovative news and public affairs programming by altering the allocative formula in favor of increased and direct grants to local public television stations. Fourth and foremost, public television's very survival was imperiled by the veto. By withholding the already inadequate monetary and linking resources, the Administration activated a series of financial crises that seriously weakened CPB's effectiveness and damaged its image. These constraints had an even more adverse affect on

PBS's budget and policy outcomes over time. From 1972 to 1976, PBS experienced a steady fall as local stations simultaneously enjoyed a real rise in monetary and discretionary fortunes.

President Gerald Ford

Under President Gerald Ford, the fortunes of the Corporation also were mixed. Support from all coalition partners, presidential, congressional, and special interests, was erratic. This period began and ended with congressional hearings in which special interest groups and several legislators openly challenged the Corporation's record on compliance with the diversity in employment, programming, and program production mandate. In response to groups representing minorities and women, Representatives William Clay (D-MO) and Parren Mitchell (D-MD) raised these concerns in the 1973 Subcommittee hearings. Subsequently, in House and Senate Labor–HEW Appropriations Subcommittee hearings Representatives Edward Roybol (D-CA) and Louis Stokes (D-OH), Chairman of the Congressional Black Caucus, as well as Senator Edward Brooke (D-MA), questioned Corporation representatives rigorously and extensively on its record of compliance with civil rights legislation.

Over the early years, public broadcasting developed a poor record of compliance with equal employment opportunity (EEO) guidelines. By 1975, only 10 percent of all public broadcasting employees were minority members. Many local stations, especially those in the southern and Rocky Mountain regions, had no minority personnel. Fifty-one percent (94 of 184) of the public radio stations and 16 percent (26 of 160) of the public television stations had no minority personnel. Most licensees that employed minority personnel assigned them to lower-level, clerical, or maintenance positions. Fifty-nine percent of the public radio licensees and 33 percent of the public television licensees had no minority staff in the officers, management, or professional categories. Even the Corporation for Public Broadcasting employed only two minority persons in the official/managerial category compared to twenty-nine whites. Minority employment in the CPB accounted for 38 percent of all employees in the less than $11,000 salary range; 23 percent in the $11,000 to $18,999 salary range; 9 percent in the $19,000 to $26,000 salary range; and none in the above $27,000 range. This issue would languish in congressional hearings until 1978.

In addition to minority employment, special interest groups were concerned with other compliance issues. Independent film producers and the AFL–CIO appealed for limits on foreign program purchases and guaranteed local union wage scales for employees of local public television stations. The FCC, National Organization of Women (NOW), National Black Media Coalition (NBMC), NAACP's Benjamin Hooks, and PBS senior officers (Ralph Rogers, Sidney James, Leonard Rosenberg, and Hartford Gunn) pressed for guarantees to women as well as minorities in programming. Even the Corporation's advisory council, ACNO, urged greater compliance with its legal mandate to promote diversity in employment and programming (Marquis, 1979, p. 25). Furthermore, Pluria Marshall of the NBMC pressed Congress to have the CPB open its then closed board meetings to the public.

The Congressional Response. On March 19, 1975, the House Communications Subcommittee held its first "overview" hearings on public broadcasting to deal with these "unanswered" questions from previous years. Representative Torbert MacDonald (D-MA) pressed the Corporation to air more local productions, increase minority and female employment, encourage more "grassroots" support for long-term financing, and open its board meetings to the public. Members of this Subcommittee also chided both the Corporation and the special interest groups to "meet among yourselves and come up with one set of figures" (ibid.).

In response to the symphony of dissent over public broadcasting, Congress proposed an appropriations bill that remained supportive of the Corporation yet addressed many concerns of special interest groups. Senator Pastore (D-RI) bound the CPB's Task Force on Long-Range Financing proposal for automatic five-year appropriations with CPB compliance to the diversity clause and civil rights legislation. As HR 6461, the bill provided the unprecedented automatic appropriation of five-year financing for public broadcasting and mandated CPB oversight and enforcement of EEO guidelines.

While HR 6461 was supported with some skepticism by the House Interstate and Foreign Commerce and the Senate Communications Subcommittees, the Labor–HEW and Related Agencies Appropriations Subcommittees maintained that automatic and long-range funding was unwise. Although public broadcasting had enjoyed unwavering congressional support for nearly eight years, the rejection of the automatic five-year appropriation signaled Congress's reluctance to give up control and oversight as well as its reluctance to set budgetary precedents and grant such spending latitude.

Subsequently, these multiple interests and issues of the coalition partners were combined in to a single compromise bill. Chairman of the House Appropriations Committee, George Mahon (D-TX), proposed deletion of the automatic appropriation in favor of three-year advanced funding voted annually. The bill also authorized five years of federal financing up to a ceiling of $88 million in 1976 extended to $160 million in 1980. These funds were to be granted through yearly appropriations and only if matched $2.50:$1.00 with nonfederal funds. Initially, 40 percent, to be raised to 50 percent, was funneled directly to local stations as Community Service Grants. Deleted by the Senate was the House provision that would have required the Corporation to oversee and enforce compliance with equal opportunity employment guidelines by the suspension of payments to stations found in violation. The compromise bill, PL 94–192, was signed by President Ford on December 31, 1975.

Although interviews indicate that President Ford was benignly indifferent to public broadcasting, the next CPB appropriation bill met with a veto. On September 29, 1976, President Ford vetoed HR 14232, the HEW appropriation bill that included CPB funding. This veto was not directed against public broadcasting. The CPB appropriation was only a very small piece of a much larger package of appropriations. Because the bill exceeded the president's target by $4 billion, the veto was a signal from the president for congressional budgetary restraint and fiscal responsibility. However, Congress overrode the veto.

Aside from the veto, there is no on-the-record opposition to public broadcasting by President Ford. Publicly, Ford never challenged the Corporation on its interpretation and execution of its mission. Off the record, however, interviews reveal that President Ford seriously considered elimination of the agency.[7] General Haig, then White House Chief of Staff, advised that "it would damage the President's image should he go on record as opposed to public broadcasting" because it was regarded as a "truly American" program.[8] Interestingly, the actual appropriations from the Ford Administration were the most generous of all. CPB appropriations were raised from $62 million in FY 1975 to $78.5 million in FY 1976 (26 percent) and $103 million in FY 1977 (31 percent). In addition to President Ford's benign indifference to public television, these nonincremental increases may also reflect Ford's weakness in confronting the overwhelmingly Democratic Congress of this period.

PHASE III: THE CARTER–REAGAN YEARS

President Jimmy Carter

On the other hand, President Jimmy Carter's Administration provided a more favorable environment for public broadcasting. Passage of the Public Telecommunications Financing Act of 1978, PL 95–567, marked an important turning point in the organization, financing and oversight of public broadcasting. President Carter established a separate Trust Fund account for the Corporation with the Treasury and eliminated the Office of Telecommunications Policy (OTP). President Carter also returned the responsibility for broadcast spectrum oversight and administration of the facilities program to the National Telecommunications and Information Administration (NTIA). For the first time, Corporation oversight and enforcement of equal employment opportunity guidelines by the Corporation were legislatively mandated. The bill also stipulated that CPB, PBS, NPR, and licensees "hold open board meetings preceded by reasonable notice to the public . . . [and that] community licensees establish advisory boards which are representative of their diverse local publics."

In the 1978 Financing Act, public broadcasting appropriations were increased substantially, from the Ford high of $152 million in FY 1980 to $172 million in FY 1982. This trend toward significantly increased appropriations resulted from strong executive and legislative support during the Carter Administration. From an analysis of CPB legislative history, it is evident that all Senate and House voting actions on public broadcasting-related issues were decisively in favor of the Corporation. From 1976 to 1982, all CPB-related bills passed, on the average, by 89 percent. (See Table 4.2.)

Even the questions posed by legislators during hearings had become quite routine. Questions were still limited to compliance with equal opportunity guidelines, the distribution of funds to public television entities, the inclusion of a culturally diverse advisory board in local station decision making, and programming trends. However, the issues of Corporation enforcement of EEO compliance and program production were only partly addressed during much of this phase. In the 1978 Public Broadcasting Act, the Corporation was further charged to conduct a special Task Force on Women and Minorities in order to assess its record on minority and female employment.

Legislative Tinkering: CPB Management Discretion. By 1978, the Corporation for Public Broadcasting had become a vastly different organization from its 1971 form. Beginning with community service grants (CSGs) in 1974, Congress would continue its piecemeal transferral of Corporation discretion over national program production and financing to the local stations. The conservative and partisan board appointments initiated by both Nixon and Ford led to the continued loss of CPB discretion over program production gained under Carter.

The Public Broadcasting Financing Act of 1978 statutorily redefined CPB policy, purposes, and activities. PL 95–567 mandated the Corporation to distribute program production grants directly to producers. In response, the CPB Board of Directors created a semiautonomous Program Fund to define the distribution criteria and to award grants to producers, including independent producers as well as local station and major production centers. Because it had no clear, consistent, or long-range objectives, Congress required the Corporation to submit a five-year public broadcasting development plan annually. This law also opened CPB board meetings to the public. With the bulk of CPB funds

Table 4.2
Coalition Support for CPB Appropriations

Year	Special Interest[a]	Executive[b]	Legislative[c]
1969	134	yes	.745
1970	51	yes	.979
1971	21	yes	.930
1972	85	no	.314
1973	47	no	.930
1974	95	no	.821
1975	122	yes	.962
1976	58	yes	.933
1977	113	yes	.928
1978	50	yes	.736
1979	51	yes	.804
1980	51	no	.991
1981	29	no	.598
1982	30	no	.644
1983	74	no	.460
1984	52	no	.750

[a]Special interest support is the total number of witnesses and submissions entered into the CPB Legislative History for an authorization hearing in a given year.
[b]Executive support describes whether an administration is on the record as favorably disposed to appropriations increases for public broadcasting. *Presidential Documents* are the sources of these data.
[c]Legislative support is the ratio of all pro-CPB appropriations' and authorizations' roll-call votes to all CPB roll-call votes for that fiscal year. For example, on Bill S.607 the yes votes were 308, the no votes were 86, a total of 394 votes. The ratio, then, is 308/394, or .781.

channeled directly to the stations, the reduction in CPB discretion, and the expanded distributive role of the CPB, the Corporation became a veritable hodgepodge of public broadcasting activity clustered under one umbrella.

Local stations most dependent upon CSGs—and to a lesser extent, state dollars—for their basic operation took few programming risks. Interviews and station statistics indicated that small state or local licensees in the southern and western regions aired no programs that used investigative reporting.[9] Managers of these stations broadcasted few or no productions of interest to local minority communities and aired more "high-brow" cultural and foreign productions. While some officials believe this programming trend reflected the different "tastes" of local publics, dissatisfied publics in some of these areas filed license challenges with the FCC.[10] From 1973–1978, the persistent public and special interest group dissent over public broadcasting's lack of accountability for civil rights regulations, employment, program production and programming underscored these flaws.

Many public groups, once staunch supporters of public broadcasting against the blandness and vulgarity of commercial broadcasting, began to express disappointment about the record of public broadcasting on programming for minorities and women, public participation in station governance, equal employment opportunity, clandestine commercialism via corporate underwriting, and the use of so many British imports (Carnegie Commission, 1979, p. 24).

President Ronald Reagan

Executive turnover once again brought important alterations to public broadcasting policy. The election of President Ronald Reagan in 1980 ushered in a new national agenda. Partly in response to the public's concern over "big" federal government, the sagging U.S. economy, and accelerated deficit spending, Reagan initiated a supply-side economic program that demanded massive cuts in government spending. The exigencies of government expenditure—defense over nondefense and mandatory programs over discretionary ones—made discretionary programs like public broadcasting most vulnerable to this new cutting mood. A similar atmosphere in Congress was kindled by the cut-oriented fiscal mood in the White House. The Corporation's budgetary and strategic management woes were only exacerbated by the new federalism, Republican congressional gains, and the Gramm–Rudman–Hollings Act.

In an analysis of Presidential documents from 1980–1986, no loss in executive support for public broadcasting during the Reagan Administration is revealed.[11] President Reagan is not on the record as an opponent of public broadcasting or its performance. He never publicly expressed dissatisfaction with the Corporation's leadership or execution of its mission. Even in his two veto messages, President Reagan voiced disagreement only with the final appropriations figures in light of the OMB's efforts to cut back programs. Although President Reagan never publicly voiced opposition to the mission of public broadcasting, he has certainly left his mark on public broadcasting policy.

"Reaganomics" and Public Television. President Reagan and his legislative coattailers were swept into office on a wave of fiscal conservatism that sought budgetary austerity and government deregulation. In an effort to reduce the deficit and spread the cuts even handedly across as many programs as possible, Congress supported PL 97–35. Under tremendous pressure from the White House, Congress passed the Omnibus Budget Reconciliation Act of 1981. PL 97–35 tied together a "multitude of benefit and eligibility changes in a single package that rewrote authorizing legislation and transformed a host of entitlement issues into

a single issue of government spending" (Chubb and Peterson, 1985, p. 26). In addition to the reductions made in a number of other programs, this Act rescinded the 1983 CPB appropriation by $35 million, from $172 million to $137 million.

Local station discretion and autonomy were enlarged substantively by PL 97–35 at the expense of centralized CPB coordination. Congress reduced the CPB board from fifteen members to ten, with two of these selected by and from public television and radio licensees. This Act also stipulated that 25 percent of the entire public television allocation be given over to the Program Fund to support programming. Congress further instructed the CPB to allocate program distribution funds (interconnection) directly to the licensees instead of passing them through PBS. Both of these allocations had formerly been internal CPB management decisions. Yet, these increased line-item allocations and the reduction in Corporation discretion failed to abate the cries of independent producers and local station managers for greater shares of the CPB budget. By the Corporation's own description

Public Broadcasting in the United States is the most decentralized, diversified broadcasting enterprise in the world. Its base and strength are the individual broadcasting stations serving their communities.

The Corporation for Public broadcasting (CPB) provides support and national coherence to public broadcasting in America. Fundamentally, the public broadcasting enterprise consists of the local licensees and the Corporation. Other national and regional organizations provide important services, without which it would be difficult, perhaps impossible, for the stations to operate or for the CPB to execute its role. These organizations were created by CPB and the stations, but literally they belong to the stations.[12]

In addition, Congress charged the Corporation to develop alternative sources of financing. PL 97–35 further authorized licensees to "broadcast announcements that use business and institutional logograms and include a reference to the location of the corporation, company, or organization involved except that such announcements may not interrupt regular programming"—limited advertising. This law also required that the CPB establish a special commission, the Temporary Commission on Alternative Financing for Public Telecommunications (TCAF). TCAF was authorized to identify an alternative method of financing public broadcasting and to conduct a demonstration program regarding advertising. This venture met with both mixed support from commercial broadcasting and mixed success from the demonstration stations. The austerity mood of the executive and Congress had culminated in the direct collection of user fees by the local stations and expanded the format for corporate underwriting. According to some observers, this "sale of advertising" has led to "commercialization" of public television (Dunagan, 1983).

Unlike other cut-oriented administrations, under President Reagan statutory modifications were incited more by economic market forces than political ones. Congress's acute need to identify programs that could be cut with minimal political costs was the aid to calculation of highest value in 1981 appropriations decision making. The Corporation was one such program in the path of the executive and legislative hatchet. Although public broadcasting enjoyed broad legislative support, there had never been any real groundswell of public support. Specialized interest groups with direct ties to the industry were public television's most ardent and active advocates. Legislative staff reported minimal public concern or involvement in public broadcasting. Congress received very little direct public feedback in the form of written or telephone correspondence from individuals concerned about public broadcasting.

Diminished Legislative Support

The 1981 decision to slash the public broadcasting budget cannot be ascribed entirely to changes in the economic environment of public organizations. Diminished legislative support was also a factor. For the first time since its inception, dissenting voices on the efficacy and magnitude of the federal role in public broadcasting were heard in the House and Senate. While legislative support for a federal role in public broadcasting had never been unanimous, dissenting legislators largely maintained a stance of quiet indifference rather than one of public opposition to a "policy as American as the flag, mom, and apple pie."[13] Although the Corporation retained strong legislative support overall, the congressional voting record on CPB appropriations bills shows some slippage. From 1975 to 1980, CPB bills passed by an average of 89 percent. From 1981 to 1985, pro-CPB appropriation bills passed by an average of only 64 percent, a loss of 25 percent (see Table 4.2).

By 1984, Republican, especially junior, legislators seized upon the changed environment of public organizations induced by "Reaganomics" to increase their own political fortunes. House Telecommunications Subcommittee minority members with heretofore minimal influence, namely, Representatives Michael Oxley (R-OH), Thomas Bliley (R-VA), William Dannemeyer (R-CA), and James Broyhill (R-NC) questioned the level of the federal involvement in public broadcasting. They also found the formerly tedious manipulations of the "too small to fuss over" CPB budget numbers very profitable.[14] Their scrutiny of the CPB budget history exposed the typically nonincremental increases public broadcasting had received over the years. Oxley recalculated the proposed CPB authorization of $238 million for 1986 from the 1985 authorized ceiling of $130 million and reported the 83 percent increase as a 90 percent increase. He subsequently executed an independent forecast and proposed an increase of $186 million, as an incremental increase of 8 percent over the 1982 figure of $172 million. Bliley characterized the 1986 CPB request as the choice between "a limousine or good solid transportation." However, Republicans and Democrats in both Houses of Congress agreed that the 1983 rollback to $130 million had been too austere.

Furthermore, Congress fully expected subsequent budget reductions to be distributed across all other federal programs as President Reagan had promised. Congressional staff maintain that the president lost considerable legislative credibility and support when he retreated from the cuts proposed for later rounds. Fearing a sustained loss of public support, the Reagan Administration backed down from many of the domestic spending cuts planned for Medicare, Social Security, and, to a lesser extent, Medicaid after the public outcry in opposition to the threatened reductions.

As the Reagan Administration retreated from threatened budget cutbacks, Congress became less attentive and less committed to White House appeals for fiscal responsibility and restraint. Neither branch was willing to bear the responsibility for the unpopular budget cuts without the complicity of the other. Neither wanted to be accountable to the middle class for having decreased its share of the federal pie. Perhaps the "blame" for public broadcasting's budgetary setback rests more with its ill-fated selection as a first-round budget reconciliation item than with the minor loss of congressional support. Had the CPB appropriation been selected for reduction in a round of budget decision making nearer the close of President Reagan's first term in office, it might have fared far better—given the Administration's progressive retreat from the unpopular budget proposals.

Role of Special Interest Groups Under President Reagan. During Phase III, special interest group support for public broadcasting also continued to decline. Even the number of witnesses who testified or presented statements at congressional hearings diminished substantially over this period. From an all-time high of 134 for the 1969 appropriation, the number of witnesses dropped to 12 for the 1986 appropriation (see Table 4.2).

There were three reasons for this diminution in special interest group support. First, the process for demonstrating public broadcasting's special interest group support became institutionalized. Only when programs or agencies were new or in jeopardy did they go through the congressional fanfare of drumming out each supportive interest to demonstrate merit, need, and public appeal at hearings. As legislative support increased, the number of witnesses needed to testify decreased. In short order, managers of the Corporation for Public Broadcasting learned the rules of the appropriations game. Public broadcasting management incorporated the participation of special interest groups so effectively that numerous and diverse advocates could be paraded on a moment's notice.

Second, the 1978 CPB board disbandment of the Advisory Council of National Organizations (ACNO), the membership group representing 78 national organizations, reduced the total number of witnesses recorded in hearings testimony. Given the routinization of the advocacy function and the increased organizational sophistication of the national public television and public radio lobby groups, NAPTS and NAPRS, it was no longer necessary for the CPB to continue the function of organizing and presenting support for public broadcasting through ACNO. Both lobbies maintained good relations with some of the representative groups so that support could be orchestrated as needed.

Third, direct support from formerly ardent advocates had fallen. Organizations such as NOW, the NAACP, and the PTA were disappointed with the record of public broadcasting on employment and programming. Only coalition partners who secured direct benefits from the appropriations remained highly supportive of public television—station managers and independent producers. Station managers were the most loyal lobbyists for public television. Other groups within the public broadcasting industry—the National Coalition of Independent Producers, the National Black Media Coalition, and Latinos in Public Telecommunications—which represent minorities, women, and independent filmmakers, became reserved and reticent supporters. Increasingly, congressional hearings testimony from members of these groups was prefaced by requests that made increased appropriations conditional upon compliance with employment and program diversity mandates.

For example, on March 15, 1988, in testimony before the Senate Sub-Committee on Communications, Arnold Torres, Executive Director of Latinos in Public Telecommunications, chided the Corporation for abject negligence of its mission of diversity in minority programming mandate. He even went so far as to request that Congress suspend reauthorization funding until the CPB devised and committed itself to a comprehensive plan for Hispanic programming and hiring. At this same hearing, an independent filmmaker, Frederick Wiseman, requested that Congress establish a line-item allocation for independent producers. (This same request had been made by another independent filmmaker, Julie Motz, at authorization hearings conducted on May 4, 1978.) These groups charged the Corporation with dereliction of its mission of diversity in programming and employment in favor of the maintenance and preservation of the public television bureaucracy, organizational survival.

Alleging that "public television is nothing more than an old boy network" or "country club for public broadcasting professionals" and the "CPB is a fiefdom for local stations" that provides "elitist programs of little or no interest to minorities," some formerly loyal special interest groups abandoned their efforts to make the CPB comply with its congressional mandate on these issues.[15] Instead, the NAACP, the National Black Media Coalition, and the National Hispanic Media Coalition elected to file challenges directly with the FCC against the renewal of licenses for several public television stations on equal employment opportunity violations.[16]

As citizen participation waned, the power, influence, and role of the station professionals, particularly station managers, steadily increased. Largely by lobbying the executive and Congress directly, public television stations increased their federal budget share. Stations received direct payments from the federal government as community service, program production, and interconnection grants. Even though the Program Fund was initially established to support independent productions, it has awarded progressively more grants to local stations than to independent producers since 1981.[17]

The Public Television Stations. The role and influence of the public television stations was significantly enlarged by the National Association of Public Television Stations (NAPTS). Prior to its name change in 1988—to the Association for Public Broadcasting—and the chartering of its representation organization, America's Public Television, Inc., in 1991, NAPTS served as the research, planning, and unofficial lobby entity for public television licensees.[18] NAPTS functioned as the sister organization to PBS and assumed the roles of spokesperson and technical expert as a regular witness for authorization hearings. In effect, NAPTS was the de facto congressional liaison for the public television stations. Most importantly, and primarily through NAPTS efforts, public television stations acquired permanent representation on the CPB board although they had been statutorily prohibited from such participation prior to 1985.

Although public television stations received 50 percent of the CPB appropriation as community service grants, in 1988, licensees ardently lobbied the Senate for even more generous direct line-item allocations. In response, the Senate proposed that 80 percent of the funds then allocated to the CPB Program Fund for distribution under open solicitation be reallocated directly to the local stations as program production grants. While the local stations lobbied the Senate, the independent producers pressured the House for the direct pass through of program production funds as a line-item allocation. Much to the dismay of all parties, the 1988 CPB appropriations hearings generated a radically different outcome.

In conference, Congress drafted a highly codified appropriations bill to quell the allegations of CPB mismanagement and address the competition over public broadcasting's benefits among special interest groups. The new bill whittled away even more CPB discretion. In the

October 1988, hearings Senator Daniel Inouye (D-HI) stated "Congress is not satisfied that the CPB has allocated sufficient funds to smaller independent producers . . . blacks and Hispanics alone constitute 30 percent of our nation's population . . . the need for programming addressing those audiences, including foreign language programming, should be a primary concern of public radio and television stations and the CPB."[19]

With passage of PL 100–626, Congress removed programming from Corporation internal budget discretion and approved additional direct line-item allocations to marginal coalition partners. A new entity, the Independent Production Service and Human Resource Development's Minority Programming Consortia, was authorized to award grants directly to smaller independent and minority producers. While the Minority Programming Consortia extended and enlarged the support of programming by, for, and about minorities, the Independent Production Service was further mandated "to make a special commitment to produce programs by and about minorities . . . [and] innovative and diverse programming geared to the child as well as the adult audiences."[20]

In sum, PL 100–626 further refined public broadcasting's mission with the insertion of a new paragraph "(6) it is in the public interest to encourage the development of programming that involves creative risks and that addresses the needs of unserved and underserved audiences, particularly children and minorities." More importantly, PL 100–626 radically "relieves the CPB board of its authority to make discretionary allocations in favor of politically prudent allocations directly from Congress."[21] This Act mandated increased CPB accountability and oversight and it stipulated the terms of compliance to these directives. The Corporation was now legally charged "to compile an assessment of the needs of minority and diverse audiences, the plans of public broadcasting entities . . . [and] prepare an annual report on the provision by public broadcasting entities . . . of service to [these] audiences" (PL 100–626).

SUMMARY

Since inception, executive turnover has profoundly influenced the strategic behavior of public broadcasting. Because performance preferences change with each administration, the organizational structure and strategic behavior of this public organization have been adjusted accordingly. Increasingly, the executive and Congress have tinkered with CPB internal management detail. As a public organization, the attainment of goals specified in the Corporation's legislative mandate has been superseded by the objective of securing increased federal appropriations. Organizational survival required compliance with the preferences and expectations of the executive and Congress, as resource suppliers and dominant coalition partners, and thereby greatly constrained public television performance.

Historically, dominant coalition partners have used public television's dependence upon federal appropriations to force its compliance and define or redefine policy. For example, in order to circumvent potential opposition to public broadcasting legislation by Congress and commercial broadcasters, President Johnson opted to delay long-term insulated financing rather than implement the Carnegie proposals that maximized future public television discretion. Similarly, Presidents Nixon and Ford altered public television organization, using threats of budgetary cutback in order to enforce their policy preferences. The budget cuts threatened by the Nixon Administration preceded and coincided with White House pressure on the CPB Board of Directors, whereas those threatened by the Ford and Reagan Administrations were directed at a much more politicized CPB board. Presidents Ford, Carter, and Reagan also increased programmatic allocations to those line items demanded by special interest groups, and thereby commensurately contracted CPB discretion.

Over the years, there has been some loss in support from coalition partners—the public, special interest groups, Congress, and the executive. Although some special interests groups have continued to provide advocacy for public broadcasting, in return for their support, these groups have competed with each other over the goals and benefits. Only those special interest groups who secured direct benefits from the appropriations have remained highly supportive of public television.

In the next chapter, the aggregate budget outcomes that result from the highly partisan legislative and organizational transformations of public broadcasting are described. The distribution of benefits is traced to the lower levels of public television organization where the winners and losers in the competition over scarce resources are identified.

NOTES

1. The Corporation for Public Broadcasting is forward funded by two years. For example, funds appropriated for 1987 provide financing for FY 1987 and give the current estimates for two successive years, FY 1988 and FY 1989. Consequently, there is a two-year lag in policy implementation as changes authorized by a given administration may not be felt until the succeeding administration.

2. Office of Education, Special Institutions, and Related Agencies Appropriations for 1973, p. 733.

3. Office of Education and Related Appropriations for 1973, p. 363.

4. The official mission of OTP was the management and oversight of telecommunications with respect to emergency planning for the military spectrum and domestic allocation of spectrum use. Three-quarters of all spectrum use is reserved for government telecommunications worldwide. One-quarter is re-

served for domestic allocation and the Public Telecommunications Facilities Program (PTFP). PTFP provides communications hardware to public broadcasting entities. Under Nixon, OTP also made telecommunications policy for the commercial and public broadcast media.

5. *Broadcasting*, August 13, 1973, p. 23.

6. See *Broadcasting*, May 24, 1971, pp. 42–43; July 3, 1972, p. 6; July 10, 1972, p. 35; July 31, 1972, p. 39; January 29, 1973, p. 60; and August 13, 1973, pp. 22–23.

7. Interview: respondent #9, 7/25/88.

8. Ibid.

9. Interview: respondent #10, 4/20/84.

10. Among them were representatives of local community groups who filed license challenges with the FCC against the Atlanta station, WETV.

11. In a prior unpublished dissertation thesis, Predilection for Predictability: An Analysis of Decision Making in Government-Financed Organizations, the author examined *Weekly Compilations of Presidential Documents* from 1967–1986 to derive a measure of presidential support. Presidential support is a categorical indicator that denotes the President's disposition toward public broadcasting as expressed in various official communications, which were recorded as either favorable or unfavorable.

12. Corporation for Public Broadcasting, *An Introduction to Public Broadcasting*, 1989.

13. Interview data. This was the most frequent response of the congressional staff interviewed (eleven out of thirteen).

14. The CPB accounts for what most OMB analysts regard as an infinitesimal portion of the federal budget. This fact has usually worked to the Corporation's advantage. "Even when the legislature is in a cutting mood, CPB gets an increase because no one wants to take the time to fuss over such small numbers." (Interview: respondent #17, 4/13/84.)

15. Interviews: respondent #1, 8/14/88; respondent #22, 10/16/84 and 5/5/89; and respondent #18, 10/16/84 and 5/5/89.

16. As of October 31, 1988, WUNC-TV (North Carolina, state system), WXEL-TV (West Palm Beach), KETS-TV (Arkansas, state system), WLPB-TV (Baton Rouge), WYES-TV (New Orleans), and WGVC-TV (Grand Rapids, MI) had FCC actions either pending or imposed against them. On November 1, 1988, the National Hispanic Media Coalition also filed a challenge to license renewal for KCET, a large public television station in Los Angeles on EEO violations.

17. See Congressional hearings testimony, Senate Subcommittee on Communications, March 15, 1988, and Table 5.2 in Chapter 5.

18. In 1988, the National Association for Public Television Stations (NAPTS) changed its name to the Association for Public Broadcasting (APB). In 1991, America's Public Television Stations, Inc., a representation organization established by APB, was recognized by the District of Columbia as a 504 C–4.

19. Congressional hearing documents. S15317. 10/7/88.

20. Ibid.

21. Interview: respondent #7, 2/18/89.

5

The Budget Outcomes: Winners and Losers

An aberration among public organizations, the Corporation for Public Broadcasting has experienced glaringly nonincremental budgetary growth. Because all public organizations must compete with each other for scarce monetary and linking resources, appropriations decision making is a very complex process. In order to simplify this process, Congress awards public organizations budget increases that generally range from 3 to 10 percent over the previous year's appropriation. Public organizations that effectively adhere to their legislative mandates and comply with the expectations of Congress and the executive are normatively and routinely rewarded with small and predictable increased appropriations. Such incremental increases permit modest, yet stable programmatic growth and adjust for inflation.

Unfortunately, this rubric is an oversimplification of a highly complex process that masks the interplay of important issues and interests—the very politics of the budgetary process. As noted earlier, the Corporation's budget increases have been preceded by significant structural overhaul or in tandem with profound policy shifts. In each instance, the examination of public broadcasting's appropriations history has shown that these modifications have been sustained largely by legislatively altering the line-item allocations for public television's redistributive components. More precisely, this history shows that increased appropriations are the outcomes of the Corporation's responsiveness to the compliance demands of the dominant coalition partners. Increased appropriations are not just simple increments that facilitate slight programmatic expansion and adjust for inflation. In return, public broadcasting, unlike most public organizations, has generally experienced radical budgetary growth over time.

In this chapter, the aggregate-level budgetary outcomes and the allocation of these funds to the lower levels of public television organization are examined. Herein, it is demonstrated that allocations to particular line items not only reflect the interests of certain coalition members, but they also flow to those members as direct benefits. In short, local station managers have wrested discretionary control and budgetary autonomy from national officials by means of community service grants. Independent producers, minorities, and women have made erratic and moderate gains as new entrants to the public television industry whereas professionals from the old vanguard of noncommercial broadcasting have become ensconced within the new bureaucracy.

As the system has expanded and line-item allocations to special interest groups have increased over the years, the likelihood of public broadcasting becoming a wholly self-sustaining enterprise has diminished. Initially, the intent of the federal role in public broadcasting was to set up noncommercial broadcasting, and then pull out. Lawmakers expected the public to finance the Corporation if public broadcasting provided resources and services valued by the public. Even in the face of rapid technological change—which has increased public television's costs dramatically—Congress expected the public to pick up the funding slack. However, direct benefits to special interest groups in the form of increased line-item allocations make this expectation untenable. The greatly expanded systems of public radio and television as well as increased direct allocations to special interest groups, especially public television stations, have mitigated against federal financing disengagement.[1]

Increasingly, Congress and the executive have encouraged and required public broadcasting licensees to generate more financing from alternative, that is, nonfederal sources. In 1981, Congress further mandated the Corporation to conduct an advertising demonstration project under the guidance of the Temporary Commission on Alternative Financing for Public Telecommunications (TCAF). Ten public television stations were authorized to air limited commercial advertising.[2] However, in 1983, TCAF concluded that none of the auxiliary revenue devices it examined would be able to generate enough revenue to replace federal funding for the foreseeable future.[3]

The appropriations history for the Corporation for Public Broadcasting is presented in Table 5.1. From this table, it is evident that public broadcasting has deviated significantly from the incremental rule of thumb. Only eight of its twenty actual appropriations have been incremental budget increases and two of those approximate zero, FY 1973 and FY 1979.[4] Although one would expect the initial years to be nonincremental given startup costs, one would not expect such persistent volatility.

Stability, if one can claim there is any, tends to follow two years behind

Table 5.1
Appropriations History for CPB ($ millions)

Authorizing Legislation	Fiscal Year	Current Dollars	Percent Change	Constant Dollars[a]
1967 Act				
PL 90-129	1968	--	--	--
	1969	5.00	--	13.89
PL 91-437	1970	15.00	200	39.05
	1971	23.00	53	55.74
	1972	35.00	52	80.05
PL 92-411 Veto:	1973	35.00	0 [b]	75.14
PL 93-84	1974	47.50	35	93.23
	1975	62.00	30	109.33
	1976	96.00	54	157.45
1975 Act	TQ	17.00	--	27.78
PL 94-192	1977	103.00	7 [b]	156.72
	1978	119.20	16	169.46
	1979	120.20	0.8 [b]	157.35
	1980	152.0	26	179.82
1978 Act	1981	162.00	5 [b]	173.54
PL 95-567	1982	172.00	6 [b]	172.00
Recision:	1983	137.00	-20	131.28
1981 Recon. Act	1984	130.00	-5	120.21
PL 97-35	1985	150.50	16	134.87
PL 98-24 (FY83 Sup.)	1986	159.5	6 [b]	139.43
PL 99-272	1987	200.0	25	171.07
	1988	214.0	7 [b]	176.28
	1989	228.0	6.5 [b]	180.94
Projected	1990	232.0	1.7	177.64
PL 100-626	1991	245.0	5.6	181.48
	1992	265.0	8.2	191.10
	1993	285.0	7.6	200.92

[a] Based on 1982 dollars using the OMB composite deflator.
[b] Denotes incremental change, between 0 to 10 percent.

presidential turnover.[5] Until FY 1988, CPB appropriations oscillate well above and below the usual incremental range of 0–10 percent. Both the budgetary outcomes and their timing show the influence of partisan politics and competition between special interest groups on policy making. For example, although the 1973 veto and subsequent partnership agreement brought increased federal funds to public broadcasting in FY 1974, they fell far short of the amount appropriated in the vetoed bill. Instead of the $65 million and the provision for long-term financing, the revised bill gave CPB $47,350,000 minus the provision.

From FY 1977 to FY 1982, the Corporation experienced budget outcomes that can be described as incremental growth. The percentage change for appropriations during this period fell within the more liberal limits of the incremental range, zero to 30 percent. PL 94–192 raised federal funding from the $88 million ceiling for FY 1976 to $180 million for FY 1980. During the Carter Administration, the actual appropriations rose from the Ford high of $152 million in FY 1980 to $172 million in FY 1982.

Passage of the 1981 Omnibus Budget Reconciliation Act (PL 97–35) halted this incremental trend and sharply curtailed CPB internal budgetary decision making. Effective FY 1983, $35 million were cut from the CPB budget. Of the balance, $5.6 million were allocated (using the CSG formula) directly to local stations as payment to the Public Broadcasting Service (PBS) for interconnection. Recipients then sent a "check twice as large . . . as dues to PBS."[6] In this way, local station managers ran interconnection through their selected representatives, not CPB. The Corporation's discretionary role was further reduced to the negotiation of the PBS annual agreement. The consummate effect of PL 97–35 was to fix the total annual payment (ceiling) for local station interconnection over time.

Officials of public television entities responded to the FY 1983 budget shock by decreasing staff and operational allocations. For example, the Corporation for Public Broadcasting's management staff experienced reductions in force—RIFs. While staff in the manager–official category dropped from 134 in FY 1982 to 102 in FY 1983 and 92 in FY 1984, minority persons in this category fell from 12 in FY 1982 to 7 in FY 1983 and FY 1984. On the allocation side, the Public Broadcasting Service and the Corporation's Human Resource Development department shares were cut to nearly one-half their prior year's allocation. In the face of this radical retrenchment, local station managers—this time led by the Rocky Mountain Corporation for Public Broadcasting—lobbied for even larger revenue shares as increased community service grants.

Under PL 100–626, the final appropriations bill considered in this book, increased appropriations were made a condition of even more strategic management and allocational changes. The trend of slowed or incremental growth was resumed for FY 1990 through FY 1993. In the main, Congress's disposition toward enhanced fiscal restraint is reflected in this Act. In the words of Representative Matthew Rinaldo (R-NJ), "the legislation before us authorizes realistic, responsible funding levels that reflect the importance of public broadcasting to our citizens. It does not promise the Moon, because we acknowledge the Moon cannot be delivered."[7] Similarly, Representative Norman Lent (R-NY) remarked, "It was difficult to believe that the committee, which approved only 1/2 to 3 percent funding increases for a variety of health programs, would approve approximately 20 percent yearly increases in CPB's funding."[8]

The distribution of the FY 1990 CPB appropriations was radically altered by PL 100–626. A new allocational formula was defined and stipulated that 75 percent of CPB interest income go to public television programming and 25 percent go to radio.[9] The Corporation also was directed to establish the Independent Production Service with an annual budget of $6 million and allocated $3 million for minority programming. By PL 100–626, statutory allocations were provided as direct line items for minority, independent, and other program production for diverse and bilingual audiences. While CPB oversight and accountability requirements were expanded under PL 100–626, FY 1990 administrative expenditures were contracted and restricted to $10.2 million plus the greater of 4 percent or a percentage equal to the Consumer Price Index in subsequent years.

AGGREGATE OUTCOMES ON ALLOCATIONS

What is the impact of these aggregate budget outcomes on lower levels of public broadcasting organization? Figure 5.1 shows that Corporation policy shifts have been achieved and sustained mainly by the manipulation of public television line-item allocations or budget shares. Budget share is the percentage funding for a particular line-item allocation of the total CPB appropriation. Over the years, all line-item allocations tend to vary with the pressure particular special interest groups bring to bear upon the congressional subcommittees responsible for public broadcasting oversight. These data highlight the tension between agency officials and local station managers over the control of public broadcasting. They also reveal the winners and the losers.

The biggest winners are the local stations. As a consequence of the 1974 partnership agreement, the Corporation's and PBS's already narrow program production roles have been reduced. Since FY 1976, increasingly larger shares of the Corporation's federal appropriations have been funneled directly to local public television stations and used at their discretion as Community Service Grants (CSGs). These direct benefits

Figure 5.1
Public Television Cumulative Budget Shares

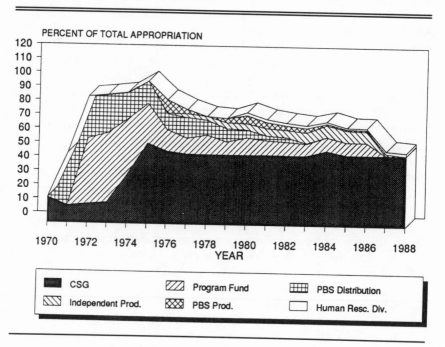

have been shifted from Corporation and PBS program production and distribution to local station managers and professionals as CSGs.

Increased CSGs are of primary interest to local station managers. Their membership organization, the Association of Public Broadcasting (formerly NAPTS), is the most vocal and dominant advocacy group for public television. During the Nixon Administration, representatives of this group actively lobbied Congress and the executive for increased and direct allocations. Although their budget share was less than 20 percent in the early days of the Corporation, CSG budget share has expanded phenomenally since the partnership agreement and PL 97–35.

Under the Nixon Administration, community service grants became a revenue-sharing device that principally benefitted more prosperous stations.[10] The more money a station raised from nonfederal sources, the more money it received from the federal government. The distributional formula was roughly: (1) "a uniform grant" for each eligible licensee equal to 0.1 percent of the total CPB appropriation for the current year plus an incentive grant derived from the CPB balance after the disbursement of all uniform grants calculated in proportion to each licensee's share of the total nonfederal financial support (NFFS) received by all such licensees in the second prior fiscal year. For example, the FY 1978 uniform grant was $119,200.00 and a station's FY 1978 incentive grant was based on its NFFS generated in FY 1976—such that a large northeastern community station generated $9,182,243.00 in nonfederal funds in FY 1976 and received an additional $1,916,130.00 as its FY 1978 CSG; whereas a small state station in the south raised $235,494.00 in nonfederal funds in FY 1976 and received $134,466.00 as its FY 1978 CSG.

Because CSGs are unrestricted grants to stations, they foster the notion of entitlement. The receipt of CSGs serve as a direct and unrestricted subsidy to local stations. Their "unrestrictedness" diminishes CPB oversight, control, and accountability. This factor lends some credence to the allegation that the Corporation is a pork barrel for special interests within the public broadcasting industry, especially station managers. In 1987, it was alleged that some station managers used these funds to decorate and furnish their executive offices and lease cars.[11] Currently, CSGs continue to receive the largest share of the CPB appropriation. (See Table 5.2.)

Program Production

Table 5.2 shows that stations received only 12 percent of CPB funds as community service grants (CSGs) in FY 1972 while CPB and PBS received 46 percent and 30 percent, respectively. Seventy-six percent of public television funding was allocated directly to these national entities for program production and distribution. After the partnership agreement went into effect in FY 1974, the CPB and PBS program production budget shares fell substantially. By FY 1976, CPB (15 percent) and PBS (11 percent) program production accounted for only 26 percent of the public television budget while direct allocations to local public television stations rose to 50 percent of a substantially larger appropriation.[12] Even monies formerly awarded to PBS for program distribution increasingly were passed through to the local stations. In FY 1984, as stipulated by PL 97-35, this role was entirely given over to the local stations.

Since FY 1974, the early claimant to substantial shares of the public broadcasting appropriation, the Public Broadcasting Service, has lost ground. In its early years, the interests of the Ford Foundation, some educational broadcasters, and producers who envisioned a highly centralized "fourth network" were reflected in PBS decision making. However, PBS budget share has declined commensurately with the influence of these early advocates. PBS management lost its credibility with the Nixon White House. With the loss in credibility came the partnership agreement and additional losses in budget share.

Table 5.2
PTV Budget Shares from CPB Federal Appropriations

Fiscal Year	Appropriation (constant $)[a]	CSG	Program Fund	Dist. PBS	Ind. Prod.	Prod. PBS	HRD
1970	39.05	18	_b	--	--	--	--
1971	55.74	12.4	--	37.4	--	--	--
1972	80.05	13.9	46.4	29.7	--	--	--
1973	75.14	15.0	49.1	26.9	--	.4	--
1974	93.23	34.6	39.4	18.7	--	.4	--
1975	109.33	57.3	28.1	16.0	--	0.	--
1976	157.45	51.9	15.1	11.3	.3	9.6	--
1977	156.72	50.1	11.0	14.6	2.8	3.0	--
1978	169.46	49.9	13.7	10.6	2.6	0.	--
1979	157.35	49.9	9.1	9.3	4.2	3.1	--
1980	179.82	49.9	12.2	5.6	4.4	5.8	2.1
1981	173.54	50.1	10.8	3.4	5.2	4.3	2.1
1982	172.00	50.0	9.5	3.2	5.2	3.1	2.0
1983	131.28	50.0	8.4	.4	7.5	3.1	1.9
1984	120.21	53.6	9.6	0.	8.6	1.0	1.4
1985	134.87	0.6	9.0	0.	8.5	.9	1.1
1986	139.43	50.6	9.0	0.	8.0	1.1	1.1
1987	171.07	50.6	--	0.	--	1.5	1.8
1988	176.28	50.6	--	0.	--	--	2.1

Source: Corporation for Public Broadcasting.
[a] Based on 1982 dollars using the OMB composite deflator.
[b] No allocation for said year.

Independent Producers

Independent producers, on the other hand, fared better. In FY 1976, independent producers secured financing from the Corporation after sustained and intensified pressure largely from the National Coalition of Independent Broadcasting Producers. Although Congress mandated neither a fixed amount nor a separate line item, the Corporation was charged to increase, guarantee, and provide an annual accounting of funds to independent producers. In response to PL 94–192, the CPB board established a "Program Fund" to contract, award grants, and support program production. Since its inception, the Program Fund has awarded program production grants to public telecommunications and public broadcasting entities as well as independent producers.

The percentages for allocations to the Program Fund and independent producers are also given in Table 5.2. Funds to independent producers are allocated as program production grants through general and open solicitation. The balance of the program production monies is awarded to public broadcasting-related entities and constitute the Program Fund category. Since 1976, independent producers have raised their budget share, from less than 1 percent in FY 1976 to 8.6 percent by FY 1984— eight times greater than the PBS program production budget share for the same year.

However, the independent producer allocation has been a somewhat fungible funding category. Funds to "independent" producers—non-station and nonpublic television-related entities—are allocated to an array of producers with varied program production capacities. Grants are awarded to one person or small shoestring production companies, fully staffed production centers with state-of-the-art equipment, and sophisticated nonprofit—typically arts, cultural or educational—organizations. Generally, grants to small production companies range from approximately $300 to $115,000. Grants to nonprofit organizations such as the Lincoln Center for the Performing Arts and the California Institute of Technology range from $100,000 to $3 million. Grants to major independent production centers such as WGBH, KQED, the Children's Television Workshop, and Family Communications can range from $1 million to nearly $6 million for some projects. Because the independent producer category includes such an array of production capabilities and capacities, this designation is misleading.

Although independent producers secured a greater number of program production grants from FY 1977 to FY 1983 than in other years (see Table 5.3), the absolute amount of these grants is less than the amount awarded to public television stations and station-related production entities. Production grants to public broadcasting-related entities range from a few thousand dollars awarded directly to small public television stations to many millions of dollars awarded to major production centers such as KQED, WGBH, WTTW, and WNET. In real terms, public television stations actually receive additional infusions of financing as program production grants. Because the major production centers and local stations consistently are awarded the largest share of program production funds, the small "independent" producers remain the most disgruntled and strident lobbyists.

Employment and Programming Diversity

Similarly, the Corporation's Human Resource Development (HRD) allocation arose as a result of intense pressure upon Congress brought by groups concerned with minority and female employment and programming. Prior to FY 1980, there was no separate line-item allocation for this unit. The promotion of minority and female involvement in public broadcasting was an ancillary task assigned to Human Resource Development. However, the Corporation was mandated by PL 95–967 to allocate funds and augment minority involvement in public broadcasting.

Table 5.3
Grants for Program Production

Fiscal Year	Prog. Fund ($ million)	Total Grants	Percent	Independents ($ millions)	Ind.[a] Prod.	Percent
1972	15.31	25	85	--	3	15
1973	16.13	40	82	--	2	18
1974	17.12	29	86	--	4	14
1975	17.44	30	83	--	5	17
1976	14.85	41	73	.35	11	27
1977	14.35	79	58	3.02	33	42
1978	19.41	68	62	3.07	25	38
1979	15.93	70	69	5.02	22	31
1980	25.20	82	70	6.67	11	30
1981	25.99	82	61	8.41	52	39
1982	25.33	103	61	8.98	67	39
1983	21.90	109	59	10.34	75	41
1984	23.72	209	81	11.24	49	19
1985	26.65	219	84	13.06	43	16
1986	27.77	224	78	13.06	62	22
1987	38.01	72	63	--	42	27

Source: Corporation for Public Broadcasting, 1989.
[a] Total grants to independent producers.

The CPB board then charged HRD to execute this task as its primary responsibility.

Since 1980, HRD has primarily provided systemwide in-service training for minorities and women, and, to a lesser extent, recruitment of new personnel. Although nearly one-third of the HRD effort (non-budgetary) has been directed toward recruitment outreach, it has rendered assistance on female and minority employment and training largely within the public broadcasting industry. In addition, HRD has assisted minority program production through the Minority Programming Consortia. It has also provided management training to local station minority and female employees through its Management Opportunity Grant Program. Moreover, these in-house programs have encouraged agency officials as well as managers of the national systems, and local stations to further supplant their minority training and operating expenditures.

Although HRD funding fell nearly 50 percent from FY 1984 to FY 1986, in FY 1987, it began to rebound. While CPB discretion over these activities, which led to cuts in HRD management and staff, was diminished by PL 100–626, funding for programming diversity was greatly increased as a distinct line-item allocation. In response to PL 100–626, the Corporation cut $2 million from HRD and other sources and reallocated these monies to minority programming and nonprogramming activities. The net effect of budget reallocations in the 1980s was to shift the responsibility for addressing minority issues from the local station managers to the purview of the Corporation's Human Resource Development department. In 1990s appropriations legislation, the responsibility for minority issues was shifted to the public telecommunications systems nationwide.

ALTERNATIVE FINANCING OF PUBLIC BROADCASTING

Counter to popular rhetoric, the greatest percentage of financing for public broadcasting has been provided by nonfederal sources since inception. Business and industry, foundations, subscribers, public auctions, and state and local governments have contributed more than 70 percent of public broadcasting's income annually (see Tables 5.4, 5.5, and 5.6). For example, in FY 1973, funding from all sources—federal and nonfederal—totaled $254,764,000. Nonfederal funding sources (NFFS) contributed $199,179,000, that is, 78.2 percent of public broadcasting's total budget. Of public broadcasting's total funds, state and local governments provided $127,275,000 (50 percent); subscribers and auctions $25,435,000 (10 percent); business and industry $9,598,000 (3.8 percent); foundations $20,181,000 (7.9 percent); and all other sources $16,690,000 (6.5 percent). The federal government contributed $55,585,000, only 21.8 percent, in direct or indirect support for public broadcasting that year.

As aggregated income, nonfederal support of public broadcasting has been consistent with congressional expectations (see Table 5.5). When federal funding decreased, the combined funding from nonfederal sources increased. In all but two areas, the percentage of nonfederal funding rose from FY 1972 to FY 1987. The percentage funding from subscriptions and auctions tripled. The percentage funding from business–industry grew threefold from FY 1973 to FY 1985 to 15.6 percent and declined slightly in subsequent years. Funding from state govern-

Table 5.4
Public Broadcasting Income by Source: FY 1972 to FY 1987 as Percentage[a]

	Federal Gov.	State	Local	Subauction	Business Industry	Foundation	Other	NFFS Total
1972	25.50	33.40	12.50	7.50	---	10.70	10.30	74.40
1973	21.80	37.50	12.40	9.90	3.80	7.90	6.60	78.10
1974	23.00	37.40	10.40	10.80	5.40	6.30	6.40	76.70
1975	25.30	34.20	8.60	11.60	5.80	7.90	6.50	74.60
1976	27.10	33.80	8.40	12.50	6.80	5.30	4.70	71.50
1977	28.00	32.00	7.60	13.20	8.30	4.70	6.10	71.90
1978	29.10	31.40	8.00	13.60	8.90	3.10	5.80	70.80
1979	27.00	32.40	7.90	14.30	9.60	3.40	5.30	72.90
1980	27.30	31.70	5.60	14.50	10.30	3.30	7.10	72.50
1981	25.10	29.40	5.70	17.00	11.30	2.50	8.80	74.70
1982	23.30	29.70	5.00	19.20	11.90	2.60	8.20	76.60
1983	18.20	29.40	4.90	21.80	13.50	2.80	9.40	81.80
1984	17.10	28.70	5.00	22.10	14.90	2.90	9.40	83.00
1985	16.30	27.30	4.70	22.60	15.60	3.90	9.50	83.60
1986	16.40	28.00	4.50	22.70	15.10	3.40	9.00	82.70
1987	18.80	25.50	3.50	23.00	15.10	3.70	10.40	81.20

Source: Corporation for Public Broadcasting, 1989.
[a] Percentage Totals reflect rounding error.

Table 5.5
Public Broadcasting Income by Source: FY 1972 to FY 1987 as Current Dollars ($ million)

	Federal Gov.	State	Local	Subauction	Business Industry	Foundation	Other	NFFS Total	Total
1972	59.812	78.315	29.390	17.610	---	25.117	24.060	174.492	234.304
1973	55.585	95.550	31.725	25.435	9.598	20.181	16.690	199.179	254.764
1974	67.005	108.706	30.350	31.618	15.555	18.429	18.722	223.380	290.385
1975	92.341	125.073	31.497	42.346	21.018	28.688	23.828	272.450	364.791
1976	130.146	112.646	34.497	54.356	29.412	23.003	20.513	274.427	404.573
1977	135.256	154.519	36.750	63.704	39.958	22.626	29.267	346.824	482.08
1978	160.762	173.946	44.237	75.216	48.970	17.213	31.981	391.563	552.325
1979	163.229	195.754	47.765	86.682	57.892	20.402	31.742	440.237	603.466
1980	192.540	223.902	39.817	102.600	72.395	23.538	50.365	512.617	705.157
1981	193.669	226.476	44.401	130.838	86.845	19.253	67.413	575.226	768.895
1982	197.625	251.771	42.353	142.076	100.486	22.108	68.403	627.197	824.822
1983	169.722	264.578	45.026	175.469	119.823	24.928	84.670	714.494	884.216
1984	166.956	279.589	48.465	192.894	144.713	27.825	91.438	784.924	951.88
1985	179.247	299.079	51.106	224.397	170.750	42.998	105.425	893.755	1073.002
1986	185.694	317.365	50.879	245.614	170.828	38.343	102.371	925.400	1111.094
1987	243.065	330.730	45.294	273.727	195.620	48.021	134.045	1027.437	1270.502

Source: Corporation for Public Broadcasting, 1989.

79

Table 5.6
Public Broadcasting Income by Source: FY 1972 to FY 1987 as Constant Dollars ($ million)

	Federal Gov.	State	Local	Subauction	Business Industry	Foundation	Other	NFFS Total	Total
1972	136.810	179.130	67.220	40.280	—	57.450	55.030	399.110	535.920
1973	119.330	205.130	68.110	54.600	20.610	43.330	35.830	427.610	546.940
1974	131.510	213.360	59.570	62.060	30.530	36.170	36.750	438.440	569.950
1975	162.830	220.550	55.540	76.670	37.060	50.590	42.020	482.430	645.260
1976	213.460	184.760	57.290	89.150	48.240	37.730	33.640	450.810	664.270
1977	205.810	235.120	55.920	96.930	60.800	34.430	44.530	527.730	733.540
1978	22.550	247.290	62.890	106.930	69.620	24.470	45.770	556.970	579.520
1979	214.040	256.690	62.630	113.670	75.710	26.750	41.620	577.070	791.110
1980	227.780	264.880	47.100	121.020	85.640	27.850	59.580	606.070	833.850
1981	207.470	242.610	47.140	140.160	93.030	20.620	72.210	615.770	823.240
1982	197.620	251.770	42.350	142.070	100.480	22.110	68.400	627.180	824.800
1983	162.650	253.550	43.150	168.150	114.830	13.890	81.140	674.710	837.360
1984	154.390	258.540	44.820	178.370	133.820	25.730	84.550	725.830	880.220
1985	160.630	268.020	45.800	201.090	153.020	38.530	98.420	804.880	965.510
1986	162.330	277.440	44.480	214.720	149.340	33.520	84.490	803.990	966.320
1987	207.910	282.890	38.740	234.130	167.330	41.080	114.660	878.830	1086.740

Source: Corporation for Public Broadcasting, 1989.

ments fell to a smaller percentage of a much larger income, from 33.4 percent of $234.304 million in FY 1972 to 25.5 percent of $1,293.988 million in FY 1987. The percentage income from the other sources category fell in the middle years, but returned to its FY 1972 level of 10 percent in FY 1987. However, funding from local government and foundations fell to within one-third of their FY 1972 percentages. Local governments, which accounted for 12.5 percent in FY 1972, fell to 3.5 percent in FY 1987. Foundation funding fell from 10.7 percent in FY 1972 to 3.7 percent in FY 1987.

In constant FY 1982 dollars (using the OMB FY 1982 composite deflator), funding from most sources has increased substantially since FY 1972 (see Table 5.6). Overall funding for public broadcasting rose by 106 percent, from $535.91 to $1,106.82 million. Federal funding changed by 53 percent, from $136.81 million to $209.91 million. Funding from state governments changed by 58 percent, from $179.13 million to $282.89 million. Subscriptions and auctions rose from $40.28 million to $254.22 million, an increase of 531 percent over FY 1972. Business and industry increased by 712 percent, from 20.61 million in FY 1973 to $167.33 million in FY 1987. Funding from all other sources changed by 163 percent, from $55.03 to $144.66 million. However, income from local governments and foundations declined by 42 percent and 28 percent, respectively. Local governments provided $62.22 million in FY 1972 and only $47.14 million in FY 1987 while foundations provided $57.45 million in FY 1972 and only $41.08 million in FY 1987.

Taken collectively, these data suggest that the funding slack caused by executive and congressional turnover and fiscal restraint is taken up largely by expanded local licensee fund-raising activity. The public, in response to the proliferation of local station subscription drives, finances public broadcasting. During the Reagan Administration, Congress and the executive expected the philanthropic and private sectors to fill the funding void imposed by the Omnibus budget cut of $35 million. Both believed that nonfederal funding for public broadcasting from these sources would increase when federal funding decreased. This has not been the case. Table 5.4 suggests that the inverse holds true. Foundation financing fell in response to the decreased federal role in public broadcasting and remains significantly smaller than that of earlier years. Although business and industry have vastly increased their funding over the years, they are far less supportive in the face of federal funding retrenchment. In general, funding from local and state governments as well as foundations is not well correlated with increases or decreases in federal funding for public broadcasting.

SUMMARY

Unlike many other public organizations, public broadcasting's budget has consisted largely of fixed-costs commitments—the maintenance, repair, and replacement of telecommunications equipment as well as multiyear contracts for interconnection and programming. Although the executive and Congress expect costs containment and efficiency, the maintenance and operation of a national public telecommunications system is a very expensive enterprise. In order to accomplish its mission and, thereby, sustain or increase audience share, public broadcasting must remain technologically competitive with commercial and cable television. Therefore, public broadcasting officials must obtain increased financing to meet the proliferative costs of the national public telecommunications system.

Public broadcasting officials have sought to increase financing from both federal and nonfederal sources to keep pace with the public television system's spiraling costs and to replenish revenue lost by fiscal retrenchment. Revenues from federal appropriations have grown at a phenomenal rate since FY 1967—by more than 52 percent in FY 1992. In general, appropriations for public broadcasting have violated the incremental rule of 0 to 10 percent increases. With the exception of a brief five-year interval from FY 1977 to FY 1982, appropriations for the Corporation have greatly exceeded this range or they have been negative, averaging 20 percent since inception.

Furthermore, funding from nonfederal sources—especially subscriptions, auctions, and corporate contributions—has increased to offset shortfalls due to the escalating costs of the system, decreased funding from state and local governments, and federal retrenchment. For example, during the Reagan Administration, Congress and the executive expected the private sector and the "public" to fill the funding gap imposed by the 1981 budget cut. Both believed that alternative financing for public broadcasting would increase as federal funding decreased. Despite limited advertising—the broadcast of announcements using logograms to reference specific organizations—and the Temporary Commission on Alternative Financing's advertising demonstration project, local public television stations remained hard pressed to expand financing from these sources.

Although TCAF and limited advertising failed to generate sufficient revenue, other fund-raising efforts have been more productive. Over the years, station managers have obtained funding from nonfederal sources that, as combined financing, has provided more than 70 percent of the public broadcasting income. From FY 1972 to FY 1987, funding from subscriptions and auctions increased threefold, while funding from business and industry peaked at 15 percent in FY 1985. However, funding from foundations and state and local governments declined substantially from their FY 1972 high of 10.7 to 3.7 percent and 12.5 to 3.5 percent, respectively.

Despite the overall increased financing, public television remains an underfunded government-sponsored enterprise. Consistent underfunding has caused persistent competition over discretion and line-item allocations among special interest groups. In the battles over public television policy, the stations have been the biggest winners. Station managers have wrested discretionary autonomy from the Corporation for Public Broadcasting and greatly increased their budget share—CSGs alone have risen from 17 percent to 50 percent. When the revenues stations receive from CSGs (50 percent of all monies allocated to the CPB) and program production grants (an average of 73 percent of all monies allocated to program production) are combined, it is clear that stations have garnered the lion's share of the public television budget. Over the years, independent producers have secured more modest funding support (an average of 30 percent of the total funding for program production) while minorities and women have made lesser gains (an average of 1.4 percent of the total CPB appropriation).

The pork barrel allegations some critics have hurled at public broadcasting are, in fact, supported by the study of the aggregate and line-item budget outcomes. Increased appropriations have mirrored the pressure special interest groups have exerted on Congress for direct benefits and enhanced control as well as system costs. In response to special interest groups, Congress and the executive have stripped the Corporation for Public Broadcasting of its internal management and budget discretion. Increasingly, federal funding has been allocated directly to those special interest groups that command congressional attention and sympathy.

More importantly, the progressive legislative tinkering with CPB internal management discretion has had profound consequences for public television performance at the lower level. A description and an examination of these effects on public television station compliance, programming, and the audience are presented and discussed in the next chapter.

NOTES

1. Similarly, the Public Telecommunications Facilities Program (PTFP) was established only to extend, maintain, and improve the quality of telecommunications services nationwide. The emphasis was on facilities improvement not ongoing systemwide subsidization. By 1983, some 75 percent of PTFP financing went to new licensees for coverage extension. These funds were used mainly to extend coverage into rural areas that heretofore lacked the capacity to transmit public broadcasting and universities that wanted to establish new stations. Only 25 percent of PTFP financing went to equipment maintenance and improvement. Interview (4/18/83).

2. The stations were WNET, New York; WTTW, Chicago; WHYY, Philadelphia; WQED, Pittsburgh; WPBT, Miami; WYES, New Orleans; WQLN, Erie; WSKG, Binghamton, New York; WIPB, Muncie, Indiana; and WKCP, Louisville.

3. See *Final Report: Temporary Commission on Alternative Financing for Public Telecommunications*, October 1983.

4. Although the advanced appropriations for FY 1990 to 1993 have been enacted (PL 100–626), these figures remain subject to revision in any budget year prior to the designated fiscal year. Since 1983, the CPB advanced appropriations usually have been adjusted annually.

5. The Corporation for Public Broadcasting is forward funded by three years. For example, funds appropriated for FY 1987 provide financing for FY 1987 and give the current estimates for two successive years, FY 1988 and FY 1989. Consequently, there is a two-year lag in policy implementation as changes authorized by a given administration may not be felt until the succeeding administration.

6. Interview: respondent #7, 2/13/88.

7. HR 10449, 10/19/88.

8. Ibid.

9. Prior to PL 100–626, CPB interest income was discretionary funding of which approximately 50 percent was earmarked for nonprogramming, that is, system support activities, for example, initiatives by Human Resource Development—such as the Minority Training Grants, employment outreach, the public participation project, and management opportunity project.

10. Until FY 1971, no CSG funds were to be used for capital expenditures. Beginning in FY 1972, grantees were allowed to use up to 10 percent of their CSG for production-related equipment. In FY 1976, the 10 percent limit was removed. Currently, stations are permitted to direct CSG funds toward capital expenses according to their individual needs. See CPB Document, Section II: CSG Distribution Criteria, p. 43.

11. Interview: respondent #7, 2/13/89, and respondent #9, 2/10/88. Also see *TV Guide*, August 1, 1987, pp. 10–11.

12. PBS budget share includes funding for program distribution and system interconnection. The budget share for these activities is denoted as the Dist. PBS column. PBS also receives production grants from the Program Fund. The budget share for this activity is denoted as the Prod. PBS column.

6

The Performance of Public Television

> "Cowboys, Caimans, and Capybaras" (*Nature*); "Mysteries of Mankind"
> (*Nature*); *This Old House*; "Ships of War" (*Discoveries Underwater*);
> "The Hidden Power of Plants" (*Nova*); *The Frugal Gourmet*; "Suspicion"
> (*American Playhouse*); "Rumpole's Last Case" (*Mystery*); "Legacy of
> the Shogun" (*Japan*); "A Waltz Through the Woods" (*Wonderworks*);
> and "Murder on the Rio San Juan" (*Frontline*)
>   PBS Top Ten Shows, April 18–24, 1988.[1]

In part, these programs constitute the federal government's return on
its investment in public television. Not only are these shows the ones
most preferred by viewers of public television for that week, they are
also representative of the programming broadcast by public television
stations during prime time in any given week. From this small sample,
it is possible to discern something about public television's performance,
provide a profile of the public it serves, and draw inferences about public
television's record on diversity in programming and employment.

However, Nielsen ratings and analyses of programming do not provide sufficient insight into the effectiveness of public television. In addition, the mission statements of the Public Broadcasting Acts are used
to identify the goals of public television and to evaluate its performance.
In order to assess the effects of expanded station discretion on public
television programming, employment, and audience diversity, this
chapter is organized into three sections. In each section, the impact of
executive turnover and aggregate budget outcomes on organizational
performance is examined.

In the first section, the focus is on public television's performance on
programming diversity. The effects of executive turnover on program-

ming are reviewed, the programming process is described, and programming trends are analyzed. In this section, it is demonstrated that programming trends arise from budgetary and employment constraints extant in the public television environment. In the next section, the goal of employment diversity is evaluated. Herein, hiring and financial statistics for a sample of public television stations are analyzed. In the last section, Nielsen–PBS audience data are used to examine public television's record of service to audiences unserved and underserved by commercial television. This chapter ends with an analysis of a randomly selected weekly ranking of PBS top ten shows.

In sum, an evaluation of the effectiveness of public television policy is presented in this chapter and answers to the following set of questions are provided: Are public television stations compliant with congressional expectations for performance? Do public television stations promote diversity in programming and employment? Why or why not? Do employment patterns constrain programming diversity? Does public television appeal to a diverse viewership? Why or why not? Who benefits from public television?

THE GOALS OF PUBLIC TELEVISION

Public television stations are both the beneficiaries and agents of public broadcasting policy. In return for the monopolistic use of the public's airwaves and federal funding, public licensees are expected to satisfy congressional expectations for mission attainment over time.[2] Legislators routinely require the Corporation for Public Broadcasting and public broadcasting licensees to verify compliance to the mandates requiring diversity in programming, employment, and audience. Therefore, these goals are used to determine organizational effectiveness and evaluate the performance of public television.

In successive statutes, public broadcasting licensees are charged to encourage "programming which will be responsive to the interests of the people ... will constitute an expression of diversity and excellence ... increase public telecommunications services and facilities available to, operated by, and owned by minorities and women ... [and provide service] to unserved and underserved audiences."[3] These goals constitute the special obligations that each public broadcasting licensee incurs in order to serve the public interest, convenience, and necessity.

To these ends, community groups, institutions of higher education, and state and local governments secure FCC licenses to operate public telecommunications entities (television and radio stations). Nationwide, there are 174 noncommercial broadcasters licensed to operate 341 public television stations.[4] Although stations vary greatly by coverage area demography, budget size, number of staff, salaries, and technical capability, each is mandated to provide programming that addresses the local tastes unique to the coverage area it serves (localism). Consequently, one expects public television stations to reflect the very diversity of American society in programming, employment, and audience in exchange for the noncommercial license as well as the sustained support from Congress and the executive.

PROGRAMMING DIVERSITY

Effects of Politics and Budget Uncertainty on Programming

As discussed in Chapter 4, under the Johnson Administration, public television's prime time audience was enlarged by the production and broadcast of cultural, educational, public affairs, and scientific programs. Until 1972, the production, scheduling, and distribution of an array of programs that appealed to a highly diverse audience was centrally coordinated by the Public Broadcasting Service. More news and public affairs programs were produced and aired by Public Television than commercial stations. These included the highly acclaimed *Washington Week in Review, Banks and the Poor, Black Perspective on the News,* and the *MacNeil–Lehrer Report.* Public television also provided more programs for audiences heretofore unserved or underserved by commercial licensees—*Sesame Street, Electric Company,* and *Zoom* for children; *Over Easy* for senior citizens; *Nova* for the science-minded; and *Masterpiece Theatre, Dance in America,* and *Soundstage* for culture buffs. Programs of special interest to minorities, for example, *Soul, Black Journal,* later *Realidades, Interface,* and *Villa Alegre,* also were produced and aired on public television.

However, the Nixon Administration brought changes in presidential preferences for the role the federal government should play in national policy generally—the new federalism—and broadcasting policy, in particular—localism and greater accountability. Under President Nixon, even "localism" took on a new meaning—greater discretion and autonomy for station managers. The policy, structure, and decision making of public broadcasting were transformed by executive turnover. The Corporation and Public Broadcasting Service's roles in nationally coordinated program production were modified by the Nixon veto. CPB appropriations were made contingent upon renegotiation of its interconnection contract with PBS. Pressured by White House staff to produce fewer news and public affairs programs critical of the Administration, the Corporation and PBS officials agreed to a partnership that made station managers largely responsible for programming discretion and interconnection.

PBS was changed from a highly centralized "fourth network" managed by national officials to a highly fragmented and decentralized membership organization comprised of public television stations. Station managers were expected to exercise discretion that was more responsive to the tastes of local audiences than national public broadcasting officials. To encourage localism, more federal dollars were passed directly to the stations as unrestricted community service grants (CSGs). These block grants to public television stations gave general managers greater control and discretion over public broadcasting policy, especially programming, purchases, and production. Modifications that were imposed by the Nixon Administration also altered the program production roles and relationships of public television stations and independent producers. Under a station-controlled PBS, the Station Program Cooperative (SPC) was established in 1974 as the principal conduit for efficiently programming public television to the tastes of local communities.

Although Presidents Ford and Carter further expanded the role of independent producers and increased federal funding for program production from FY 1975 to FY 1980, these gains proved temporary. Subsequent budget cuts introduced by the Reagan Administration in 1981 further enlarged the role stations played in program production while they diminished the role of independent producers. As the line-item budget analysis in Chapter 5 shows, nonsolicitation grants from the Program Fund increasingly were obtained by the public television stations. Initially established to augment program production by independent producers, from FY 1984 to FY 1986, public television stations and their related production entities annually received approximately 81 percent of the more than 200 grants awarded by the Program Fund.[5] By pooling production monies, activities, and expertise, station managers offset programming problems caused by inadequate federal funding and escalating production costs.

No longer exempt from the harsher realities of the budget process, the decade of slowed CPB growth greatly altered public television programming. In spite of the trend toward appropriations increases, which averaged 40 percent from FY 1967 to FY 1981, federal funds remained insufficient for the technologically demanding and capital-intensive nationwide system of public broadcasting. Costs due to system maintenance, expansion, upgrading, and operations have continued to outpace funding from all sources over the life of the Corporation for Public Broadcasting.

Thus, changes in policy preferences, caused by executive turnover and imposed as budgetary constraints, had tremendous impact on public television's ability to achieve the diversity in programming mandate. The Public Broadcasting Service's role in the production, distribution, and scheduling of national programming was altered by the reorganization stipulated by the revised partnership agreement between CPB and PBS. At the same time, these changes were harbingers of continued reductions in direct discretionary allocations to PBS. Changes in policy preferences also brought a progressive decline in support from public broadcasting special interest groups. In addition to lobbying Congress, some independent producers, minority and women's groups, and labor unions withdrew their support from public broadcasting.[6]

The Public Television Programming Process

In order to minimize programming costs and fill the national schedule, public television station managers increasingly have found it more efficient to pool programming resources and purchase programs from abroad.[7] As the cost of producing one hour of prime time public television approaches $200,000 per show, few station managers or independent filmmakers have the capability or capacity to develop, promote, and distribute high-quality programs independently.[8] Therefore, the Station Program Cooperative, foreign coproductions and purchases, consortium productions, major PTV production centers, and public television-related entities have emerged as the primary sources of programming.

The Station Program Cooperative (SPC)

From 1974 through June 1990, the Station Program Cooperative was a pipeline for public television programming. The SPC was established as a cost-effective method for purchasing and distributing programming that satisfied the unique tastes of each public television station and its public. Born of the need to offset budget shortfalls initiated by the Nixon veto, PBS devised a new marketing system for programming. The SPC enabled the nation's public television stations to cooperatively select and finance national programming distributed by the Public Broadcasting Service.[9] This PBS-administered programming system permitted public television stations to pool their resources and, thereby, fund nearly half the National Program Service.[10] Some of the programs funded and distributed by the SPC included *Sesame Street, Nova, American Playhouse, Nature, The MacNeil/Lehrer Newshour,* and *Great Performances.*

Through the SPC, a democratic program selection process was instituted whereby public television station managers actually determined programming for a given broadcast (SPC) year. Each Summer, PBS staff convened an annual Programming Fair where a panel of station officials made final programming decisions. Proposals from independent producers and public television stations were solicited and compiled by PBS for station consideration. Each station representative voted on every program proposal in a preference round held each Spring. Some seventy proposals were pared down to thirty-five to forty proposals. These were subsequently screened and reviewed by the panel of station officials at the Programming Fair. The panel's final selections were added to the national programming schedule.

In June 1990, PBS national program financing and management were restructured. The SPC was replaced by the National Program Service. Under this new model, programming decision making was placed under the control of the Chief Programming Executive, who is advised and assisted by the PBS National Program Service Advisory Committee. The Committee has thirteen members appointed by the Chief Programming Executive chosen from a field of public television programming professionals and independent producers. The National Program Service is an effort to pool funding, reduce the costs, and eliminate duplication in the provision of programming for the national schedule.

Both the SPC-assisted and programming now provided by the National Program Service as well as all other programs that constitute the national programming schedule are supplied through one of the following production arrangements: local, major, consortium, foreign, international coproduction, independent, or commercial. When stations broadcast syndication reruns such as *Lawrence Welk*, *The Saint*, and *Lassie*, the sources are described as commercial. When stations broadcast programs produced in their own facilities, they are considered local productions. However, these same programs are classified as major public television productions when produced by KCET, KQED, WTTW, WGBH, WQED, WNET, or other public television productions when produced by smaller public television stations.[11] Foreign productions are shows produced abroad and acquired for broadcast by a particular station. Many of these "acquisitions" are then distributed throughout the system by the purchasing station.

Consortium production describes both multiple sponsorship for a single production team and several producers for a single program. Some consortium productions are produced by independents and stations either in collaboration with, under the auspices of, or by contract with major public television production centers, for example, Boston's WGBH, Los Angeles' KCET, and New York's WNET. *Wonderworks* and *Frontline* are examples of consortium productions. International coproduction describes shows produced by a public television station and a foreign producer. Series such as *Nature, Discoveries Underwater, Nova*, and *Japan* are produced by major public television production centers (WNET, WGBH, WQED, and WTTW) in collaboration with foreign producers.

Some of the larger public television stations—generally, those with budgets over $4 million—and independent producers have formed public television-related production entities to produce major programs and series. The Southern Educational Communications Association (SECA, comprised by South Carolina public television stations) and Public Television Playhouse, Inc. (comprised by WNET, WGBH, and KCET), are examples of such entities. These entities secure funding from federal and nonfederal sources through open solicitation grants and solicited contracts. For example, Public Television Playhouse, Inc., is contracted by the Corporation for Public Broadcasting to produce the drama series *American Playhouse*. Programs furnished by public television-related production entities are classified as independent productions.

Public television stations can obtain programming from these sources in several ways. Stations can air programs purchased from the SPC— now the National Program Service—that are then simultaneously transmitted throughout the system by PBS. Stations can air programming acquired from other producers or film houses (domestic or foreign) as canned footage upgraded to meet PBS specifications. Stations can broadcast reruns syndicated by commercial networks. Stations can also purchase programming produced by a station, consortium of stations, or station in collaboration with independent or foreign producers.

Public Television Programming Trends

Public Television Programming by Production Source. An analysis of public television programming by producer source shows the effects of public broadcasting's politicization, subsequent reorganizations, and budget cuts on programming diversity. Table 6.1 gives the total percentage hours from each producer source that were broadcast from 1974 to 1986, and reveals several programming trends. These trends demonstrate that budgetary uncertainty has constrained public television performance in three critical ways: First, stations have become more reliant on foreign productions because they are cheaper than domestic ones. Second, programming produced by local sources (stations) has declined. Third, program production by major public television stations has remained nearly constant over time.

In Table 6.1, the major and other public television producer categories show a slight decline in the total percentage hours broadcast during this period and the local and Children's Television Workshop (CTW) categories show steady reductions. Major and other public television sources accounted for 45.5 percent in 1974 and fell to 40 percent in 1986. Productions from the CTW and Family Communications have fallen from 22 percent in 1974 to 14.7 percent in 1986. However, the total percentage hours for foreign, largely BBC, productions has doubled since 1974.[12] Foreign and international coproductions were 5.8 percent of the total broadcast hours in 1974 and accounted for 13.3 percent in 1986. Yet, even these figures understate the true level of foreign production (a

Table 6.1
Programming Content by Source

Program Content	Percentage Total Hours by Year						
	1974	1976	1978	1980	1982	1984	1986[b]
Local[a]	11.4	10.1	7.7	7.0	6.7	5.7	5.6
Major PTV Center[b]	(45.4)	21.5	24.2	28.4	25.9	(44.4)	8.1
Other PTV Center		26.7	28.0	17.8	19.7		31.9
		(48.2)	(42.2)	(46.2)	(45.6)		(40.0)
Consortium	2.5	1.7	1.8	2.7	2.6	3.3	c
CTW/Family Com.	22.0	18.0	16.8	17.1	15.8	16.4	14.7
Independent	5.9	6.1	5.3	7.9	11.3	9.2	10.7
Commercial	1.9	2.8	2.7	3.2	3.9	2.8	3.2
Foreign[d]	(5.8)	(7.6)	(9.1)	7.8	6.0	8.9	8.9
Int./Coprod.				4.7	4.1	4.3	4.4
				(12.5)	(10.1)	(13.2)	(13.3)
Other	5.1	4.6	4.4	3.5	4.0	4.6	3.6
Non-PTV/ITV[e]	--	--	--	--	--	--	8.7

Source: PBS Research Division, 1989.

[a] When a survey respondent (station) participates in an international coproduction, the source is coded "local." Nonparticipants code it as an international coproduction.

[b] Major PTV producers include WTTW, WQED, WNET, WGBH, WETA, MCPB, KQED, and KCET from 1974–1984. In 1986, it is restricted to WNET and WGBH. Other PTV source includes other PTV stations (not local or major) and PTV-related production entities. Data for these categories are merged in some years. These are given in parentheses.

[c] In the 1986 survey, the consortium category is added to the other, commercial, and independent categories.

[d] Foreign and international coproduction categories are disaggregated for some years. Consistent with the prior computation, the sums are given in parentheses.

[e] This category is introduced in 1986. It includes cable productions.

trend also noted by Hitt (1987) in his critique of PBS programming for the week of November 21–28, 1987).[13]

Moreover, coding changes introduced in the 1986 survey inflate the percentages for local and other public television centers and deflate the percentage for major centers. The designation, major public television center, is restricted to productions supplied by WGBH or WNET. Prior to 1986, productions supplied by WTTW, WQED, WETA, KQED, and KCET were coded as local by the producer or acquisition station and coded as other by stations that broadcast them. Collectively, these changes obscure industrywide concentration effects among the larger stations that accompany economies of scale.

Table 6.1 further suggests that the broadcast of programming from independent and commercial producers varies with the political and budgetary dynamics of public television.[14] Programming from independent sources rose with increased allocations to the CPB Program Fund. In 1974, four grants were awarded to independent producers, while the Program Fund was allocated $17.12 million and the total percentage hours broadcast from independent sources was 5.9 percent. By 1982, independents were awarded 67 grants, while the Program Fund was allocated $25.35 million, and 11.3 percent of the total hours broadcast were provided by independent producers.

Moreover, the total percentage hours broadcast provided by commercial sources is inversely related to line-item increases. Commercial fare accounted for 2 percent of the total percentage hours broadcast in 1974 when Program Fund allocations were low. This percentage rose only slightly as the allocations increased, and doubled when the allocation was cut to $21.90 million in FY 1983. Subsequently, the broadcast of commercial fare declined as Program Fund allocations were restored in 1985.

Table 6.1 also indicates that public television stations have tended not to use the increased community service grants primarily to produce and broadcast their own programs. Despite the inflated percentage due to coding, in 1986, local productions were aired at a rate less than half that of the percentage total hours broadcast in 1974, down 5.6 percent from their all time high mark of 11.4 percent. Although this may be attributed to increased production costs, this diminution in local production continued to fuel allegations that public television stations used these monies to supplant other expenditures.[15]

Public Television Programming by Type. Executive turnover and budget uncertainty also have affected programming diversity by modifying the type of shows produced and broadcast. In response to pressure from the Nixon Administration, from 1973 until 1982, PBS took fewer programming risks. Fewer PBS recommendations for production grants were accepted by the CPB.[16] Of the production grants PBS recommended

Table 6.2
Programming Content by Category[a]

Program Content	1974	1976	1978	1980	1982	1984	1986
General	61.6	66.5	70.7	71.3	72.0	73.0	59.7
News/Pubs. Affs.	12.6	11.9	11.0	12.2	12.4	14.1	16.7
Information/Skills	15.6	19.9	23.6	22.8	24.5	25.5	29.5
Cultural	17.9	20.9	22.1	21.9	22.8	20.1	13.1
General Childrens	10.7	10.0	8.7	8.9	7.5	7.9	b
Other General	4.4	3.8	5.3	5.5	4.8	5.5	4.3
Instructional							25.4[b]
Adult	1.9	1.4	1.2	1.0	1.4	.6	b
Sesame Street[c]	36.4	33.0	29.8	29.2	27.7	17.2	14.1

Source: Katzman and Katzman, *Public Television Programming by Category*, 1984, and 1986; unpublished survey data furnished by PBS Research Division.

[a] Percentage total hours.

[b] In the 1986 survey, the categories are redefined. These categories are collasped into other categories and cannot be decomposed.

[c] Includes *Sesame Street*, *Electric Company*, *Villa Alegre*, and other instructional programs for children and youth until 1982. The *Electric Company* and *Villa Alegre* went out of production after 1982.

and the CPB approved, the overwhelming majority were cultural and scientific, not news or public affairs. PBS distribution of national public affairs programming was reduced because station managers' requests for these programs declined in response to their alleged antiadministration tone and lack of appeal to local audiences.[17]

The most severe setback from the Reagan budget cuts was borne by the children's category. In FY 1981, *The Electric Company* and *Sesame Street* went out of production altogether. After considerable public dissent was brought to bear upon Congress, funding was restored for production of the highly acclaimed and highly regarded *Sesame Street*. Despite funding restoration, Table 6.2 shows that overall children's programming has declined steadily. Instructional children's programming fell from the high of 22.5 percent in 1974 to 14.1 percent in 1986, and general children's programming fell from 10.7 percent in 1974 to 7.9 percent in 1984 (the last year for which these data are disaggregated).[18]

Table 6.3
Percentage Programming About Minorities

DAYPART	PERCENTAGE
Before 9 A.M.	15.5
9-12 P.M.	25.2
12-3 P.M.	9.8
3-6 P.M.	29.5
6-Prime	12.8
Prime	4.4
After Prime	2.9

Source: PBS Research Division, 1986.

Table 6.2 also reveals a slight decline in news and public affairs broad-casting and a steady rise in information and skills programming, that is, how-to shows.[19] Meanwhile cultural programming has fluctuated, falling to an all time low of 13 percent in 1986. How-to shows, especially culinary, fix-it, and hobby, have proliferated since 1978. For example, in 1989, on any given Saturday, twelve culinary shows were broadcast over the District of Columbia's coverage area alone (three by WMPT-TV, four by WETA-TV, and five by WHMM-TV). These and other in-formation and skills programs filled 16.5 hours of this area's Saturday carriage schedule for that year.

Minority Programming. Although the early years of public television were noted for diverse minority programming such as *Realidades, Villa Alegre, Interface, Soul, Big Blue Marble*, and *Electric Company*, the produc-tion and broadcast of minority programming have declined substantially since 1980. In an unpublished segment of the 1986 CPB public television programming survey, data also were collected from public television stations on the broadcast of minority programming (see Table 6.3). Of the 9,202 programs aired by broadcasters in 1986, the majority, 75.5 percent (6,951), seldom featured members of minority groups.[20] Of these, 82.2 percent aired no programs produced by or about minority persons. Of the 17.8 percent that broadcast programs produced by or about minorities, most (73 percent) were children's shows and were aired during nonprime time. Of the stations that aired programming about, that is, featuring, minorities, 71 percent of these shows were for children, 26.8 percent were for adult viewers, and the balance (2 percent) were intended for teens and children.

Evaluation of Public Television Programming Diversity

Many broadcasting professionals, media analysts, and special interest groups are disappointed by public television's record of performance on the programming diversity mission. Some have labeled public television programming as bland and elitist. Others claim it has failed to live up to expectations for diversity and excellence in the face of political and budgetary constraints. Most agree that public television's attainment of this goal is limited in three important ways: by pooling production and increasing foreign imports, by bland programming, and by pandering programming to donors. In order to fill the national schedule with cheap and high-quality programming—competitive with commercial and cable television—it is necessary to pool program production, which leads to less innovative and more "tried and true" fare, and to import substantial footage from abroad. To obtain funding from corporate underwriters and politicians, domestic producers of public television fare avoid controversial topics and issues. To increase funding from the "audience" or "public," station managers provide programming that reflects the preferences and demographic profile of a narrowly defined group of viewer checkwriters—subscribers to public television.

When the SPC was established, some public broadcasting critics feared that the diversity of public television programming would suffer at the expense of participation in the programming process—localism. The cooperative was viewed as "a giant step toward true local control of the national schedule . . . stations themselves now select—with their dollars—much of the national schedule. What some question is whether this cooperative will also produce excellence and diversity to match its democratic virtues . . . will [stations] tend to select programs of mass appeal, and neglect programming for special interest."[21]

Some public broadcasting critics and officials say these fears have been realized. On the eve of public broadcasting's twentieth birthday, Jack Hitt, associate editor for *Harper's Magazine,* asserted that "this prime time lineup is no cause for rejoicing. It is not so new and creative as it is cheap."[22] Hitt credits the underfinancing of public television as the cause of its "bland homogeneity . . . many programs in the *Nature* series use canned footage produced by foreign filmmakers, purchased at low cost, and upgraded (voiced over) for American audiences." Of the programming scheduled for the week of November 21–28, 1987, Hitt found that thirty-one of the eighty-four hours were foreign productions.

Foreign productions have become the linchpin of public television's national prime time schedule. Limited by the preferences of corporate underwriters and politicians, public television station managers are compelled to import programming. Foreign acquisitions and production deals with major public television producers provide the means for filling the public television broadcast schedule given PBS budget constraints. According to one PBS official, "the only way to fill up the schedule is to use acquisitions. [Foreign productions] may be taking U.S. money away from U.S. producers, but [public television] can't survive without coproduction deals and acquisitions."[23]

Furthermore, public television station managers' dependence upon tax and corporate monies limits programming diversity. The need to avoid controversial programming and the need to raise production funding abroad also encourage the use of British producers. Independent producers and PBS officials report that "[producers] can't raise production monies from U.S. corporations on controversial issues . . . the British houses are the best producers in the world . . . they provide high quality films [and] are not reluctant to fund ethnic and controversial projects. . . . It is much easier to raise money to produce films abroad. Without the BBC, you wouldn't have the series, *The Africans*."[24]

Producers, media critics, and underwriters readily acknowledge that corporate funding is inextricably linked to noncontroversial and conservative, if not blatantly bland, programming. A 1987 survey conducted by *TV Guide* critic John Weisman also found that corporate underwriting constrains programming diversity. He cites an award-winning producer who admitted that "corporations fund me because I put them alongside Mom and apple pie and the American flag. And so I won't do controversial shows."[25] Hitt also maintains that "PBS delivered itself into a more refined bondage: corporate sponsorship" (*Harpers*, 1987). Furthermore, in a 1986 study of public television in the United States and Great Britain, the BBC's Committee on Financing concluded that corporate underwriting of U.S. public television tended to bias funding toward noncontroversial projects and programs (Weisman, 1987).

A poignant example is afforded by Gulf and Western. When New York's WNET aired "Hungry for Profit" from the series *Nonfiction Television*, the corporate underwriter, Gulf and Western, withdrew financial support from the station. The show argued that multinational corporations, including Gulf and Western, buy up huge tracts of land in the Third World to produce food for export (ibid.). Then Gulf and Western Chairman and CEO Martin S. Davis wrote a letter to WNET President John Jay Iselin calling the program "virulently antibusiness if not anti-American." In this letter, Davis concluded, "we cannot support Channel 13."

Some public broadcasting officials also maintain that public television programming does not reflect the diversity of American society. These officials say that programming reflects the tastes and interests of the predominantly white male public television station managerial hierarchy, not the demographics of the coverage area.[26] As in commercial broadcasting, programming decisions are made by a professional and technical managerial hierarchy void of minority input. Seldom do station managers survey their coverage areas to ascertain the programming preferences of the local residents.

In public television, programming discretion is the province of the general, programming, and operations managers of public television stations. These managers are businessmen whose primary concern is the profitability of the station. For these managers, public television's "viewer checkwriters" are "the audience."[27] These managers perceive the heaviest public television viewers as subscribers who are college-educated, high-income, and nonblack professionals. Station managers also claim this audience prefers intellectually challenging programming that consists mainly of nature, culture, and drama shows. Increasingly, station managers pander prime time pledge week and season programming to the tastes of these donor viewers who comprise only 9 percent of all television households.[28]

Consequently, the "bland homogeneity" and "elitism" of public television programming are attributable to the need to raise funds as well as established employment patterns within public broadcasting. Frequently, station managers nix program purchases and feeds that they believe to be either offensive or unappealing to donor viewers. For example, managers of Cleveland's WVIZ opted not to broadcast the nationwide feed of a highly acclaimed program about negative racial stereotypes of African Americans, *Ethnic Notions*. Irrespective of Cleveland's ethnic diversity and substantial black population, WVIZ's managers stated that the program was "too distressing to local audiences."[29]

Analyses of public television employment statistics show that minority persons hold fewer than 5 percent of the stations' managerial positions nationwide. Because African, Asian, Hispanic, Native American, and other ethnic minorities play a minor role in public television station management discretion, one cannot expect programming to reflect this diversity.[30] Managers make decisions based on their experiences, values, beliefs, and knowledge. The more homogeneous the managerial hierarchy, the less likely that programming decisions will reflect ethnic diversity. Therefore, established employment patterns, which allegedly rely upon the male-dominated old-boy network within the broadcasting industry, also constrain programming diversity.[31]

EMPLOYMENT DIVERSITY

Given the mission of public broadcasting and the role employment patterns play in programming diversity, let's look at public television's performance on the diversity in employment goal in greater detail. Over-all, the analysis of public television stations' employment data demonstrates that stations are compliant with congressional expectations for employment diversity. However, stations exercise considerable autonomy over the definition of compliance. Public television station managers are free to define both the terms and direction of compliance. Although managers have exercised high total compliance, they have hired far more women than minorities. When aggregated, total compliance (the employment of females and minority persons) is substantial and even-handed across all stations by license type, budget size, and geographic region. Total compliance for the sample stations ranged from 25 to 45 percent. When the data were disaggregated, station managers exercised compliance by employing a significantly higher percentage of women than minority persons. Nearly half of the sample stations employed no minority persons as managers or officials.

The Public Television Station Sample

In order to assess compliance to the diversity in employment mandate, a sample of thirty-four public television stations was identified. A public television station is the broadcasting unit that transmits a single non-commercial television signal on a single channel. Each station has its own transmitter, channel number and call letters; and each serves a community covered by the broadcasting radius of the transmitter.[32] Of the thirty-four stations, twenty-seven were in operation long enough to furnish the necessary financial and employment statistics. Data were obtained with the consent of individual stations and provided by the Corporation for Public Broadcasting. The financial data are reported for FY 1970 to FY 1980 and the employment data are reported for FY 1977 to FY 1979.[33]

The sample was randomly selected on the basis of region, budget size, and license type. Region differentiates public television licensees by the time zone, membership in a neighboring network, and the noninter-connected broadcasters for a particular geographic area. The regions are northeast, central, south, and west. Budget size describes four budget categories created on the basis of CPB-adjusted budget figures from the Public Television Financial Summary.[34] The categories are

Under $800,000
$800,000–1,599,999
$1,600,000–3,999,999
Over $4,000,000

Public television stations are also distinguished by the type of license issued by the Federal Communications Commission. An FCC license is held by either a community, university, state, or local broadcaster. A community licensee is an independent foundation or corporation free from government or institutional financial affiliation. A university license is held by institutions of higher education (university, college, junior, or community college). A state license is held by state authority, agency, board, or commission or multiple-station state system. A local licensee represents a station licensed to a local school board, district, or authority.[35] Of the 174 noncommercial broadcasters, 49 percent are community, 32 percent are university, 13 percent are state, and 6 percent are local licensees.

Hypotheses. In exchange for federal financing, one expects public television licensees to exhibit compliance with congressional requirements for employment diversity. One expects some variation in public television station compliance by region, type, and budget size due to demographic factors and established societal patterns of discrimination. For example, public television stations in or near large urban and ethnically diverse cities should employ more women and minorities. Because these groups have historically low participation rates in mid- and senior-level management positions, compliance is measured as the mean employment rate for women and minorities in the official-manager category from FY 1977 to FY 1979.[36] One also expects those public television stations with high percentages of federal income to be more compliant with congressional expectations for employment diversity.

Findings. Analysis of employment data for the sample shows public television stations are compliant with congressional expectations for employment diversity in the aggregate. However, these data also reveal significant differences between minority and female employment. From 1977 to 1979, 48 percent of the sampled stations employed no minority persons in the official-manager category. Of the total sample, females accounted for 26.7 percent and minority persons were 4.5 percent of this category.[37] This trend toward the employment of substantially more females than minority persons persists across all comparisons: region, license type, and budget size. This disparity also persists over time.

Among the regional comparisons, the west showed the least disparate compliance between women and minorities.[38] Females were 17.6 percent of the employees in the official-manager category and minority persons were 6.1 percent. Of the seven stations in the west group, four employed no minority persons and the balance averaged 14 percent. In the south, 27.4 percent of these employees were women and 5.7 percent were minorities. In the northeast, 34.5 percent were women and 2.3 percent were minorities.

Analysis of employment diversity by budget size shows that public television stations with the largest total budgets exercised more balanced compliance behavior. Stations with budgets greater than $4 million maintained staffs comprised, on average, by 28 percent females and 11 percent minority persons. Stations with budgets less than $4 million employed significantly more females than minorities.[39] Of these, 54 percent employed no minorities at any time during the ten-year period. Stations with budgets under $0.8 million maintained staffs comprised 20 percent by women and 2.6 percent by minority persons.

When the stations were compared by type of license, once again compliance is skewed toward females. Holders of local and state licenses employed moderately more females than minorities in the official-manager category, 34 percent to 8.3 percent and 21.2 percent to 6.2 percent, respectively. However, community and university licensees employed substantially more women than minority persons, 29.5 percent to 3.9 percent and 20.6 percent and 3.1 percent, respectively.

In exchange for federal financing, one also expects those public television stations with high percentages of federal monies to be most compliant with the diversity mandate because they are more dependent upon this income source. Stations with budgets greater than $4 million receive federal funds, as CSGs, which average 6 percent of their total income. Moreover, managers of these stations tend to view the federal contribution as marginal because they are not as dependent upon federal financing. One manager from this group maintains that federal income is "really a small percentage," "we could do with it or without it," and "more trouble [with respect to coalition members' demands for accountability] than they are worth."[40] Stations with budgets of less than $4 million, however, average 39 percent federal income. Therefore, stations that receive federal funds in excess of the mean percentage federal income of 22 percent are expected to have higher rates of compliance than stations that receive less.[41]

The expectation that stations receiving more direct federal funding are more compliant with the diversity in employment mandate was not well confirmed by analysis of the data.[42] Variation on compliance by the mean percentage federal income was not systematic. Seventy-eight percent ($n = 9$) of the stations with more than 22 percent CSG income employed no minority persons in the official-manager category. One station employed neither women nor minorities, although it derived 21.4 percent of its income as CSGs. Stations with less than 22 percent ($n = 18$) CSG income employed, on average, 5.8 percent minorities, and 33 percent of these stations employed no minorities as managers.

More important, for stations with budgets greater than $4 million, the actual federal payment, in fact, is substantial. Such stations received approximately 6 percent of their income from the federal government— the average value of the federal CSG payment to these stations ranged from $0.5 million to $1.5 million. On the other hand, stations with budgets under $0.8 million received payments that averaged from $155,128

(87 percent) to $599,120 (21 percent). In absolute terms, although 6 percent may seem inconsequential, large stations are unlikely to decline the millions they receive. Although smaller stations receive higher percentages as CSG funding, both large and small public television stations are dependent upon this income source.

With respect to the attendant objective of increased minority ownership, public television's performance has been poor. As of November 1989, only eight stations were minority controlled.[43] Seven were not part of the contiguous United States—and four of these were U.S. territories. Of the minority controlled public television stations, two were African-American, two were Hispanic, three were Asian, and one was Native American. In other words, 2 percent of the 327 public television stations were controlled by minority licensees.

AUDIENCE DIVERSITY

Over the years, the CPB and PBS have assembled audience data that describe who watches, who gives, and what is viewed on public television. However, these data are subjected to various interpretations by broadcasting professionals and critics. Some officials emphasize a diverse and growing public television audience, whereas station managers highlight a rise in membership, PBS ratings, and audience cumes.[44] Yet, critics note that public television maintains a small and stable audience share, 9 percent of U.S. households.

However, these data are biased by the very programming broadcast on public television and they ignore important distinctions in the definition of audience. Foremost, programming—what is broadcast—determines viewership as well as giving. Those viewers who choose public television can express preferences only from the menu (carriage schedule) offered by stations. Hence, television viewing is program-dependent. Secondly, official interpretations of these data confound distinctions that underlie the operational definition of audience: the characteristics of heads of households in which public television is viewed versus the characteristics of those who actually watch, and the cume (viewing public television for six or more minutes) versus average minutes per viewing household.

Viewer Checkwriters As Audience

Budgetary constraints, programming trends, and employment patterns also affect public television's effectiveness in serving unserved and underserved audiences. As station managers become more dependent upon subscribers as a funding source (Chapter 5), they increasingly gear programming to the tastes of "upscale" viewer checkwriters. By narrowly targeting programming to donor viewers, audience diversity is diminished because fewer of the TV households that do not fit the upscale member profile watch public television. Therefore, public television programming assumes the quality of a self-fulfilling prophecy.

Pledge week programming provides a salient example. For several years, demographic analyses of public television membership have identified subscribers largely as nonblack, college-educated, higher-income, and highly skilled—upscale households. Station managers also have attributed a high and positive relationship between membership and viewing frequency.[45] They have concluded that the public television audience is made up of donor viewers (members) who prefer challenging programs. Hence, managers select shows for pledge week that narrowly target this group of member viewers. Therefore, station managers pursue a marketing strategy whereby programming reflects neither the diversity of American society nor the demographics of the particular station's coverage area. Instead pledge week programming is likely to be dominated by nature shows with a few culture and drama programs.

Analyses of black philanthropy and scrutiny of PBS audience data suggest that this strategy may be misguided. Analysts of philanthropic organizations as well as legislative staff and officials of public television have noted the failure of development officers to target minorities in fund-raising campaigns.[46] The problem, as these observers see it, is not that minorities fail to give, but that fund raisers fail to ask. A 1988 Joint Center for Political and Economic Studies survey of black philanthropy supports this claim (Carson, 1989). When asked, especially through work-site charitable deduction plans, 63 percent of blacks ($n = 643$) compared to 55 percent of whites ($n = 695$) made substantive charitable contributions (Carson, 1989, p. 27).

Public Television Audience Composition

From the television demographic data regularly compiled by A. C. Nielsen, one also discerns a number of characteristics that describe the public television audience. Table 6.4 presents the demographic breakdown for a sample of 1,200 heads of households where public television is viewed for 6 or more minutes per day (cume). The demographic profile for the heads of households with the heaviest viewers is consistent with the "upscale" description given by station managers. During prime time, on average four to thirty-two more minutes of public television are

Table 6.4
PTV Audience Demographics Season-to-Date (October–March 1988)[a]

	PERCENT DISTRIBUTION		PTV AUDIENCE		INDEXED TO U.S.[b]		PENETRATION[c]		AVG MIN PER VIEWING HH	
	U.S. TVHH (000)	%	FULL DAY	PRIME	FULL DAY	PRIME	FULL DAY	PRIME	FULL DAY	PRIME
All TV Households	88,660	100.0%	100.0	100.0			56.2	32.3	179	100
Persons 2+	229,120	100.0%	100.0	100.0			40.7	21.6	133	87
Head of Household Demos										
Race										
Black	9,560	10.8%	8.6	7.6	80.0	70.0	44.6	22.2	169	83
Non-Black	79,040	89.2%	91.4	92.4	102.0	104.0	57.4	32.8	180	101
Education										
Lt 4 yrs. HS	21,860	24.7%	22.2	22.0	90.0	89.0	49.8	27.9	160	87
4 yrs. HS	31,790	35.9%	35.3	32.4	98.0	90.0	54.5	28.2	146	87
1-3 yrs. College	16,010	18.1%	18.0	17.7	100.0	98.0	55.3	30.5	179	95
4+ yrs. College	18,940	21.4%	24.5	27.9	114.0	130.0	63.3	40.7	226	119
Occupation										
Prof/Owner/Mgr	20,180	22.8%	24.8	26.3	109.0	116.0	60.7	36.4	205	105
Clerical & sales	13,480	15.2%	14.1	13.0	93.0	85.0	51.7	26.8	159	84
Skilled & Semi-Skilled	28,770	32.5%	30.7	25.4	94.0	78.0	52.7	24.6	154	80
Not in Labor Force	26,170	29.5%	30.5	35.3	103.0	119.0	57.6	37.4	187	114
Income										
Less than $10,000	15,320	17.3%	14.8	13.2	85.0	76.0	47.8	24.3	150	80
$10,000-$19,000	18,160	20.5%	18.3	19.1	89.0	93.0	50.1	29.4	174	106
$20,000-$29,999	16,070	18.1%	17.6	17.2	97.0	95.0	54.3	30.0	158	96
$30,000-$39,999	13,410	15.1%	16.2	16.0	107.0	106.0	60.0	33.4	182	90
$40,000+	25,640	28.9%	33.0	34.5	114.0	119.0	63.9	37.8	207	110

	(000)	%[a]								
County Size										
A	36,930	41.7%	43.9	45.6	105.0	109.0	59.2	34.9	190	102
B	26,660	30.1%	28.9	29.6	96.0	98.0	54.1	31.4	185	107
C and D	25,010	28.2%	27.2	24.8	96.0	88.0	54.2	28.0	157	86
Cable										
Non-cable	43,910	49.6%	49.5	52.9	98.0	105.0	55.5	33.7	211	113
Pay Cable	25,340	28.6%	27.6	24.2	102.0	89.0	55.7	27.7	149	81
Basic Cable	19,350	21.8%	22.9	22.9	103.0	103.0	58.3	33.0	154	92
Persons Viewing										
Kids 2–5	14,170	6.2%	8.4	3.9	136.0	63.0	55.3	11.2	207	46
Kids 6–11	20,190	8.8%	8.6	5.1	98.0	57.0	39.7	12.2	102	49
Teens 12–17	19,880	8.7%	5.3	4.1	62.0	47.0	24.6	9.9	74	49
Women 18–34	33,970	14.8%	11.1	9.9	75.0	67.0	29.9	13.9	121	65
Women 35–49	24,180	10.6%	10.1	10.4	96.0	98.0	38.3	20.4	115	82
Women 50–64	17,000	7.4%	9.0	11.1	122.0	150.0	48.5	30.8	145	98
Women 65+	16,750	7.3%	9.3	11.9	127.0	163.0	50.4	33.6	164	109
Men 18–34	33,560	14.6%	12.0	11.4	82.0	78.0	32.8	16.1	95	65
Men 35–49	23,110	10.1%	10.8	12.9	107.0	128.0	42.6	26.6	109	78
Men 50–64	15,130	6.6%	8.3	10.5	126.0	159.0	50.1	32.7	141	105
Men 65+	11,180	4.9%	6.8	9.6	140.0	197.0	55.8	40.6	178	123

Source: Nielsen Television Index.

[a] Percentages may not sum to 100% due to rounding.

[b] "Indexed to U.S." represents the demo's PTV proportion relative to the household/person universe.

[c] Penetration % is the weekly cume for each specific demographic group.

viewed in households headed by persons with incomes greater than $40,000 or more than four years of college.

However, these same data also indicate that persons not in the labor force actually view more minutes of public television. From October to March 1988, data for heads of households show that persons not in the labor force viewed nine more minutes than professionals, thirty more than clerks and sales persons, and thirty-four more than skilled workers. Whereas data for the actual viewers show that more men and women aged 65 and over view more minutes during full day and prime time than any other subgroup. Among all age groups, children aged two to five years are the heaviest full day viewers—with 207 minutes. In other words, when one examines data for persons actually viewing public television, the heaviest viewers are children and senior citizens—persons not in the labor force. However, one cannot develop a more detailed profile for those who actually watch public television because demographic data are not provided for these data subsets.

Similarly, when one examines the data subset that describes the relative size of the public television audience, the upscale profile of the public television audience does not surface. Contrary to station managers' claims, persons who attain high school levels of four years and less constitute the largest audience segment, 58 percent for full day and 54 percent for prime time. By audience size, again persons not in the labor force are 30 percent (full day) and 35 percent (prime time) of the public television audience. Thirty-three percent of the audience have incomes less than $20,000. Although more women and men aged 18–34 watch during the day, we do not know their employment status. However, children comprise most of the full day public television audience, 17 percent.

In short, one cannot define the public television audience as primarily upscale. There is a tremendous difference between the profiles suggested by demographics for the heads of households in which public television is viewed and those given by the persons who actually watch. The heaviest actual viewers of public television and the largest audience are children and seniors or persons not in the labor force.

Viewing is Program-Dependent

More important, Nielsen data for audience composition also indicate that public television viewing is program-dependent. For example, the smallest recorded audience segment was comprised by African-American viewers. Although African-American viewers watched 169 average minutes during full day and constituted 9 percent of the public television audience, this audience segment increased noticeably when minority programming is aired. Two series, *Eyes on the Prize* and the *Africans*, netted larger African-American audiences, 22 percent and 11 percent, respectively. Also more African-American viewers watched *Victory Gardens* (14 percent), classical music programs (11 percent), and certain specials, for example, *Championship Skating* (14 percent), *Holiday Entertainment/Jimmy Stewart* (17 percent), and the *Entrepreneurs* (15 percent).[47]

Additional support for program-dependent audience demographics is provided by a recent PBS study of member viewing habits.[48] The study examined the popular attribution by station managers that there is a high correlation between membership and members' program preferences. It also tested whether members' program preferences differed from those of general U.S. television households. Data on television viewing were collected from 1,811 public television station members in four markets (WQED/Pittsburgh, KTCA/Minneapolis–St. Paul, KAET/Phoenix, and KOAP/Portland, OR) and 3,486 persons from the Nielsen general TV audience pool.

The study's findings were mixed but illuminating. Consistent with station manager's claims, the study found that members viewed more hours and gave higher ratings to public television fare than persons in the general sample. It also found that members were older, more highly educated, and watched less television than the general TV audience. However, the study showed that members preferred news and public affairs programs, whether commercially or publicly provided, and rated commercial ones higher than those supplied by public television.

More important, members—just as the general TV audience—use public television as a source of programming secondary to the commercial networks. Even though public television programs received higher ratings among members, twenty-two of their twenty-five most popular shows were commercial. While *Cosby* and *60 Minutes* tied for the highest rating, *Murder, She Wrote* and *Cheers* ranked third and fourth. Even programs produced by public television stations as local productions earned higher ratings from members. In addition, the Discovery Channel, CNN, Financial News, and Arts and Entertainment drew larger cumes among members.

These findings suggest that public television primarily serves underserved audiences. Viewers, whether members or nonmembers, use public television programming to enhance the overall television menu. Members and the general TV audience watch the same fare. Although members show lower overall television usage, they—like the general audience—shop around and sample programs from commercial, cable, independent, and public television.

SUMMARY

In this chapter, an assessment of public television performance on three goals is provided: diversity in programming, diversity in employment, and audience diversity. Executive turnover and budget uncertainty have transformed public television from a centralized organization managed by national officials into a highly fragmented and decentralized—loosely coupled—system directed by the stations. Changes in presidential preferences for public television performance, imposed by manipulating the Corporation for Public Broadcasting's budget, have determined public television performance over time. The executive's use of budget sanctions, congressional tinkering in CPB allocations, and sustained underfunding have exerted substantial impact on the organizational effectiveness of public television.

Indeed, the list of Top Ten Shows presented at the beginning of this chapter is instructive. Of those ten most heavily viewed programs, none was produced by minority producers. Though three were produced by independent producers, two of these were collaborations with major public television production centers (WGBH and WNET), and one was produced by a public television-related entity (Public Television Playhouse, Inc.). Five were programs from series produced by major public television centers and foreign producers—international coproductions (WGBH, WTTW, and WNET) and two were station productions (WTTW and WGBH). One was a foreign production—acquired and distributed by WGBH. Of these ten top shows, six were categorized as information and skills, two were dramas, one was news and public affairs, and one was general.

In short, this profile describes an audience most interested in nature shows. It describes programming that is oriented mainly toward those who are information and skills. It also describes programming whose employment patterns primarily benefit major public television stations and foreign filmmakers.

Foremost, budgetary factors have constrained the types of programs produced, supplied, and broadcast on public television—programming diversity. In the face of public broadcasting's escalating technical demands and costs, stations have pooled their production activities and monies. Pooling resources, as public television-related production entities, has enabled public television stations to produce better and higher-quality programs at lower cost. Increasingly stations have been more competitive with independent producers for CPB production grants. By pooling, station managers have secured larger production grants in open solicitation and as solicited contracts. By pooling, the public television stations have been the big winners in the battle over production funding.

Budgetary uncertainty also has led station managers to import more foreign fare while it has discouraged diverse, innovative, and creative local programming—risk taking. Station managers produce, acquire, and air programming that is safe, bland, and homogeneous—geared to a narrowly defined audience of upscale viewer checkwriters. In order to obtain funding from corporate underwriters, producers of public television fare also avoid controversial issues. While the quality of all public television programming has improved, there is less programming targeted to unserved audiences. The percentage of children's programming produced and aired has decreased. There have been fewer programs for senior citizens. Programs produced by or about minorities have also declined. (Although a number of programs still feature minorities, these are largely children's shows.)

On the employment diversity goal, public television stations are compliant with the congressional mandate for employment diversity overall, but managers exercise considerable latitude. Most stations employ significantly more women than minorities in managerial positions. Moreover, many stations employ no minority persons as managers or officials, and little, if any, pressure is exerted to bring them into compliance. Inadequate federal funding has left accountability to the same actors who are charged with policy implementation: the managers of the public television stations. Although the CPB is charged with oversight and enforcement of equal employment opportunity guidelines, it has no resources or capacity to do so. Consequently, the CPB is forced to rely upon the public television station managers for fulfilling and reporting compliance with the employment diversity mandate.

Budgetary constraints, programming trends, and employment patterns also inhibit public television's effectiveness in serving diverse audiences. In a hierarchy where minority persons hold fewer than 5 percent of the discretionary positions, management is more sensitive to budgetary concerns than diversity issues. As station managers become more dependent upon subscribers as a revenue source, they progressively pander programming to the tastes of "upscale" viewer checkwriters. Audience diversity diminishes because television viewing is program-dependent and fewer nonupscale households watch and support public television. As station managers proliferate programming that is safe and targeted toward a narrow audience segment, public television viewership takes on the quality of a self-fulfilling prophecy. Those who watch, give.

More important, viewer checkwriters as well as the general audience use public television as a secondary source of programming. Viewers, whether members or nonmembers, use public television to augment the commercial, cable, and independent television menus. Although members show lower overall television usage, both audiences watch the same fare.

In the next and final chapter, the resource dependence and rational models of organizational theory are applied in order to evaluate public television. Some policy prescriptions are provided. The implications of this evaluation for public broadcasting in particular, and public policy in general, are considered. In conclusion, the preeminent question posed by the title of this book is answered.

NOTES

1. Top Ten Shows (ranked by Household Cume percent), April 18–24, 1988, *National Audience Report*, Public Broadcasting Service, 1988, p. 3.

2. R. H. Coase, 1959, "The Federal Communications Commission," *Journal of Law and Economics*, 2(10): p. 14. Also Smith, 1973, and Noll et al., 1973.

3. Public Laws 90–129, 95–567, and 100–626.

4. Number of licensees and stations current as of March 1990.

5. See Table 5.2. Station-related production entities are consortium arrangements or organizations comprised by stations and independent producers. These entities are also classified as independent producers by CPB, PBS, and other public broadcasting professionals and, thereby, are eligible for monies from the CPB Program Fund. Some of these entities, for example, National Educational Television (NET), Southern Educational Communications Association (SECA), and Public Television Playhouse, Inc., have become principal providers of domestic program production.

6. See Chapter 3.

7. Public television stations have also engaged in broadcasting-related ventures to raise revenue. For example, some stations operate commercial radio stations (Chicago Educational Television Association, which holds the noncommercial license for Chicago's WTTW-TV, also owns commercial radio station WFMT-FM). Some stations rent their production facilities; others produce, acquire, and distribute programs; and a few sell publications spun off from broadcasting activities, for example, WTTW-TV's *The Frugal Gourmet* and WFMT-FM's *Chicago* magazine.

8. Interview: respondent #4, 5/31/89.

9. See Public Broadcasting Service, *Program Producer's Handbook*, January 1989.

10. When the SPC was in effect, the National Program Service consisted of the prime time schedule, children's block, Saturday "How To" block, and the fringe time feed of PBS. It was the major and most visible service of PBS.

11. In FY 1986, major public television source was redefined as either a WGBH or WNET production. Shows produced by all other public television stations are classified as local productions.

12. Data for the foreign and international coproduction categories are merged for the early years—from 1974–1978, but decomposed from 1980. Decomposition suggests stable resource allocation and use over time. However, summing these data, which is consistent with prior record keeping, shows a significant and steady increase in the use of foreign productions.

Coding variation in the foreign category over time and the designation of the U.S. producer of a series, which is internationally coproduced, as local or major source undercounts the true level of foreign productions. Because the major and local categories do not identify those segments of a series that are produced abroad, it is difficult to ascertain the true percentage of foreign productions.

13. Jack Hitt, *Harpers Magazine*, November 1987, p. 58. Coding inconsistencies noted in the previous note also play a role here.

14. Also see John Weisman, 1987.

15. Ibid., p. 11.

16. See Carnegie Commission Report, 1979, p. 48.

17. Ibid. Also see Cater and Nyhan, 1976, and Rowland, 1976, p. 126.

18. Although the number of children's shows has declined, the quality of these productions has improved significantly. Children's fare has become very glitzy and more expensive. Interview: respondent #3, 7/24/89.

19. Programming data are unavailable for years prior to FY 1974.

20. A program featuring minorities is one that has a member of a minority, racial, or ethnic group who appears in the show. 6,951, that is, 75.5 percent of all programming, aired less than the annual average featuring members of minority groups. However, the "annual average of programs featuring minority groups" is not specified in these data. This item was coded as "yes" or "no," where "yes" describes equal to and greater than the annual average.

Programming about minorities includes shows produced by or about persons from minority racial or ethnic groups.

21. Gunn, 1974, p. 16.

22. Jack Hitt, 1987, p. 58.

23. Interview: respondent #3, 7/24/89.

24. Ibid.

25. John Weisman, 1987.

26. Interview: respondent #3, 7/22/89.

27. Interviews: respondent #7, 2/13/89, and respondent #3, 7/22/89. Also see Jack Hitt, 1987, p. 58.

28. Ibid. and *National Audience Report*, PBS, June 24, 1988.

29. Interview: respondent #18, 5/5/89.

30. Interview: respondents #3, 7/24/89; #18, 5/5/89; and #22, 5/5/89.

31. Ibid.

32. See Nathan Katzman and Solomon Katzman, *Public Television Programming Content by Category FY 1982*, p. 1.

33. Employment data are reported biennially in the Public Television Financial Summary published by CPB. These data are collected by the authority of the FCC and there is approximately a one-year lag from the time of submission to availability through the CPB.

34. The CPB uses six categories to describe the budget sizes of public television stations. These are collapsed into four in order to accommodate the statistical demands imposed by sample size. See Katzman et al., 1982, p. 2.

35. Ibid., p. 3.

36. See Chapter 3 for the rationale.

37. In 1977, the CPB commissioned the Task Force on Minorities in Public Broadcasting to assist "in the development of policies that maximize the growth, development, employment, and participation of minorities in all aspects of public broadcasting." The commission found that, from 1972 to 1978, 33 percent of all public television stations had no minority staff in this category. Minorities accounted for 4.7 percent of all employees in this category and females were 10.5 percent.

The t statistic calculated for the sample indicates a significant difference between the employment percentages for women and minorities in this category ($t = 5.11 > 0.001$).

38. $t = 2.76 > 0.01$.

39. $t = 5.78 > 0.001$.

40. Interview: respondent #11, 4/19/84.

41. The percentage federal funding for public stations in this sample ranged from 6 to 87 percent.

42. The Pearson Product Moment Correlation indicated no relationship between federal income and compliance.

43. KHET and KMEB/Hawaii, KVZK/Pago Pago, KGTF/Guam, WHMM/Washington, D.C., WTJX/Virgin Islands, WIPR and WMTJ/Puerto Rico, and KYUK/Alaska.

44. Cume defines the percentage of viewers who watch public television for six or more minutes at a time.

45. PBS, *A Study of Member Viewing Habits*.

46. Interviews: respondents #23, 10/13/84, #22 and #18, 10/11/84. Some CPB officials and legislative staff have suggested that PBS assemble a pledge week carriage schedule that appeals to a broader audience—one that includes minority, senior, and female as well as upscale segments—and that station managers pitch their fund-raising efforts to include all these segments.

Also see Emmett D. Carson, 1989.

47. See *National Audience Handbook*, PBS Research, January 15, 1988.

48. Public Broadcasting Service, 1987.

7

Panacea, Pork Barrel, or Public Trust?

Public television is a panacea. Public television is a pork barrel. Public television is not a public trust. Although some of the early advocates of public broadcasting legislation sought enactment as a public trust, because public broadcast licensure grants rights of domain over the private use of the public airwaves, such legal status was never conferred.[1] Instead, the Corporation for Public Broadcasting was established as a government-sponsored enterprise, a private nonprofit government organization that supports the nationwide public telecommunications systems of television and radio. Despite a history of politicization, budget uncertainty, and compromises, public television is a successful enterprise that yields greater benefits than costs.

Legally mandated to provide a dependable vehicle for the transmission of high-quality cultural and informational programming that serves the public interest, convenience, and necessity, the Corporation for Public Broadcasting was designed to afford something for everyone. The Corporation's mission was intentionally ill-specified to encompass the disparate goals of all decision participants and to accommodate the interests of all relevant constituencies. The telecommunications industry, private philanthropy, educational broadcasters, influential citizens, and the mass public all benefit from public television. While noncommercial broadcasters have secured a federally protected and funded environment for public television, the public has received programming that would not have been provided commercially.

In this final chapter, we return to the rational and resource dependence models of organization theory to answer the question posed by this book. Although each model uses different criteria and suggests divergent assessments of public television performance, we show that survival needs are superseded by rationality norms and strategic behavior is determined by the need to retain coalition members. Compelling explanations of strategic behavior in public organizations are provided by highlighting public television's responsiveness and adaptiveness to its dynamic and uncertain environment. This chapter not only provides an evaluation of the effectiveness of public television, it also gives an assessment of the net effects of the competition over priorities, means, and ends under uncertainty. This chapter and the book are concluded by some policy prescriptions for public television, public organizations, and public policy decision makers.

ORGANIZATION THEORY REVISITED

As stated in the opening chapter, the criteria used to evaluate organizational effectiveness are derived from two perspectives. The rational model is generated by the closed systems perspective and the resource dependence model is generated by the open systems perspective. According to the rational model, organizations are closed determinate systems in which decision makers exercise control over goals, structure, means, participants, and technology through strategic management. Herein, organizational performance is determined by well-defined goals and means, sound management practices and plans, clear channels of communication and lines of authority, and standard operating procedures. Herein, organizational effectiveness is the attainment of specified goals by improved efficiency—minimized cost and maximized gain.

Alternatively, in the resource dependence model, organizations are defined as open and adaptive collectivities, within an uncertain and dynamic environment, that are comprised by coalitions of special interest groups with shared purposes. According to this model, decision makers set goals, manage ties of mutual dependence, and regulate exchange transactions in order to secure stable and predictable flows of the requisite resources—means, materials, and technology. Herein, organizational survival is assured by the management of mutual dependence, which results in the retention of coalition partners, and the regulation of exchange transactions. Herein, organizational survival is organizational effectiveness.

The Models Contrasted

Different criteria and divergent assessments of organizational effectiveness are suggested by each perspective and each model. The attainment of well-defined goals is stressed by the criteria of the rational model, whereas organizational survival is stressed by the criteria of the resource dependence model. Where the policy analyst ascertains abject failure by imposing the rational model, he or she can pronounce unqualified success by imposing the resource dependence model. Where the same analyst highlights public television's record of poorly defined goals, gross inefficiency, mismanagement, excessive fragmentation, and overbureaucratization by imposing the rational model, he or she can highlight its broad policy appeal, legal autonomy, decentralized discretion, sustained coalition support, and appropriations fortunes by imposing the resource dependence model.

Such contrasts illustrate that much of the criticism media analysts level against public television arises from the application of the rational model. When the criteria of the rational model are applied to the performance of public broadcasting and other public organizations, most policy analysts are hard pressed to explain these organizations' continued survival. How can an organization that frequently garners disparaging national headlines—such as "paradise postponed," "highbrow pork barrel," "a name without a concept," "public broadcasters looking for a sure thing," and "why it's time for public television to go private"—continue to obtain substantially increased appropriations over time. Pragmatic explanations, such as "government agencies hardly ever die" (Kaufmann, 1976), successful use of the "Washington Monument Game" (Wildavsky, 1979), and constituency politics, are insufficient.

However, the body of knowledge on performance in public organizations is enhanced by an application of the resource dependence model. More comprehensive explanations of effectiveness are provided by this model because the focus is on the public organization's unique attributes, the legislative mandate and federal funding. In the public organization, decision makers must routinely alter the goals, means, and domains in order to secure resources critical to survival. Decision makers also must demonstrate that the public organization is compliant with congressional, executive, and special interest group performance expectations in order to retain continued support and the flow of resources these groups supply. In return for increased appropriations, the public organization is made more vulnerable to the uncertainties and complexities of political market forces than economic ones. By focusing on each entity's history of appropriations and adaptation to the compliance demands of coalition members as suggested in the resource dependence model, the policy analyst can make more complete and useful evaluations of performance in the public organization.

Imposition of the resource dependence model takes into account the public organization's budgetary and political uncertainty in a competitive environment. Analyses of the Corporation for Public Broadcasting's appropriations history coupled with its record of coalition formation and retention present a picture quite different from that offered by many policy analysts. Hardly the ineffective and inefficient public organization that is depicted by the rational model, public broadcasting is highly successful and secure. Although public television is greatly under-funded, when compared with commercial television or in light of public broadcasters' more ambitious technological and programming objectives, after all is said and done, public television decision makers do a decent job of managing its budgetary fate.

PUBLIC TELEVISION PERFORMANCE AND STRATEGIC BEHAVIOR IN PUBLIC ORGANIZATIONS

Over the years, the strategic behavior of the Corporation has largely involved coalition formation and retention. Utilization of these strategies is consistent with the basic tenets of the resource dependence model. As discussed in Chapter 1, in this model, it is maintained that managers of the effective organization strive to reduce reliance upon a single supplier and stabilize the flow of critical resources—developing alternative suppliers. Managers also try to incorporate the needed resources within the organization in order to minimize the attendant loss of discretion and autonomy, diminish dominance by particular actors, stabilize the resource exchange, and, thereby, reduce uncertainty.

Strategies That Reduce Uncertainty

Generally, decision makers in public organizations can choose any one or a combination of strategies to reduce uncertainty. Organization officials can employ a buffering strategy, whereby the required resources are accumulated as large inventories or stockpiles. Or officials can negotiate mutually beneficially deals with resource suppliers—the bargaining strategy. If the interdependencies cannot be regulated or managed by buffering or bargaining, then officials can try to extend the organization's boundaries to incorporate the uncertain or unreliable units by cooptation, vertical integration, or coalition formation. The use of these strategies permits officials to modify the organization's ties of mutual dependence and, thereby, regulate exchange transactions.

Cooptation (Selznick, 1949) describes the process of absorbing new members into the leadership or decision structure of an organization in order to avert threats to stability or survival. In the case of public broadcasting, this is exemplified by the extension of CPB board membership to public television and station representatives. Vertical integration (Thompson, 1967) refers to the incorporation of successive stages of production within the organization. In this instance, each stage of production uses as its resource inputs the product of the preceding stage and produces resource inputs for the next stage. In public television, the Public Broadcasting Service (PBS), which funds, schedules, distrib-

utes and transmits programs broadcast on public television stations, is
an example of vertical integration.

Coalition formation (Thompson, 1967; and Pfeffer and Salancik, 1978)
is a form of joint venturing where special interest groups come together
to pursue a shared goal as a unified entity. In public broadcasting, the
coalition formation strategy was used to enact the Corporation for Public
Broadcasting as a government-sponsored enterprise. As long as officials
satisfy the demands of coalition members, the coalition remains in force
(coalition retention) and organizational survival is guaranteed.

Coalition Formation and the Public Organization

Public organizations are greatly constrained in their capacity to utilize
strategies that modify ties of mutual dependence and regulate transactions by developing alternative suppliers. Because agency officials are
limited, by legal mandate, in their choices of alternative suppliers, pro-
cesses, and methods, generally two courses of action are possible for
the public organization. Both are variants of coalition formation. Officials
in public organizations can exercise exclusive dependence on one or
more actors—namely, Congress and the executive—then adhere to their
performance expectations and request only modest increments in the
budget appropriations.

Or, when the public organization's legal mandate so stipulates, bureaucrats can develop multiple resource suppliers. For example, in quasi-
government or government-sponsored organizations, bureaucrats have
the discretionary and budgetary autonomy to determine both the suppliers of the requisite resources and the terms of compliance. Bureaucrats
in most government-sponsored enterprises are free to "find the ways
and means to finance programs 'off budget' " as long as they are in
accordance with presidential preferences (Seidman, 1988). Fannie Mae,
the Securities Investors Corporations, and the Corporation for Public
Broadcasting are examples of government-sponsored enterprises that
operate outside the established legal system. In these organizations,
bureaucrats may regulate transactions by forming coalitions with multiple resource suppliers and by managing existing ties of mutual dependence through compliance to Congress, the executive, and special
interest groups—coalition retention.

Public broadcasting bureaucrats and station executives have pursued
both strategies. These decision makers have generated funding from a
multiplicity of sources. Diversification, joint ventures, and pooling production activities have been highly successful strategies. Station executives also have intensified fund-raising efforts among viewer
subscribers, business and industry, state and local governments, and
foundations—as revenue alternatives to federal financing. Managers of

the Corporation for Public Broadcasting have also strengthened existing ties to special interest groups by assuming the formerly contested role, as providers of supportive services to the public telecommunications systems.

Coalition Retention: Special Interests Matter

To say that "special interests matter" in government decision making is an understatement. Foremost, in public organizations, decision makers must maintain support from the special interest groups that coalesced to enact the federally protected environment and secure stable resource exchange. In public organizations, decision makers cannot rigidly adhere to a fixed set of goals or an ideal organizational form. In exchange for resource inputs, public organizations are responsive to the demands of coalition members. In a complex, uncertain, and competitive environment, the preferences and priorities for organizational performance are typically disparate. To survive, managers of public organizations, such as the Corporation for Public Broadcasting, must cater to the demands of dominant coalition members—Congress, the executive, and the more influential special interest groups, particularly, station managers.

More than any other goal, decision makers in public organizations pursue survival. The public organization's mandate is subordinate to securing increased appropriations from one year to the next. As a consequence, public organizations are malleable because agency officials implement whatever forms, roles, and missions the dominant coalition partners prescribe. Policy goals initially stated in the public organization's mandate are diluted. Just as the demands of Congress and the executive are altered by political turnover, the strategic behaviors of public organizations are also responsive to the winds of political change. As public organizations undergo appropriations decision making over time, line-item budget allocations are frequently tinkered with and mandates and missions are amended. Therefore, in the public organization, the need to survive the upheavals of changing political preferences assumes primacy.

Since inception, public broadcasting has been very vulnerable to budgetary, partisan, and special interests politics. Usually, public broadcasting decision makers have coped with this uncertainty by redistributing its line-item allocations in patterns consistent with the demands of the dominant coalition members. Hence, decision makers have repeatedly redefined the Corporation's mission, structure, and means in order to survive, that is, in order to sustain stable and increased annual appropriations. Over the years, the efforts of public television managers to satisfy Congress, the executive, and influential special interest groups have generated the "pork barrel" allegations. Although the search for organizational survival has diluted the goals of public broadcasting and consequently constrained the effectiveness of public television, the support of dominant coalition members has been maintained over time.

Public broadcasting bureaucrats play delimited roles in the strategic management of public television. These agency officials are more peripheral participants in the policy-making process because they are largely agents of the special interest groups—principally, the public television station executives and station membership organizations. As agents of the dominant coalition, public broadcasting bureaucrats are charged to provide coherence to public broadcasting in America by executing the expectations and demands of the dominant coalition members. These agency officials, like those in other public organizations, can confront formidable resistance to policy implementation when their aims are inconsistent or incompatible with the demands of the more active and involved special interest groups. This constrained role is an outcome of public broadcasting's history of discretionary fragmentation, diminished autonomy, and politicization.

Whereas bureaucrats play a prescribed role, the public is almost incidental to public broadcasting policy. Citizen participation is primarily proxied by the special interest groups. Despite the citizen involvement implied by its name and occasionally urged by Congress, public television encourages about as much "public" participation as commercial television. With the exception of direct financial appeals—subscription campaigns and auctions—little effort is made to promote public participation.

Aside from the Nielsen ratings (based on a sample of 1,200 households metered overnight) and infrequent audience and donor surveys—often used to justify the Corporation's pleas for increased federal funding—the public has little formalized opportunity to express its preferences for public television. In the absence of formal avenues for participation, it is difficult for the public to impart its preferences because the public tends to be uninformed about the organization and mission of public television. What voice the public has is expressed by a few and usually brokered by more marginal special interest groups like the now-defunct Advisory Committee of National Organizations (ACNO), the National Black Media Coalition, and Latinos in Public Telecommunications.

Let's Make A Deal

The Corporation for Public Broadcasting, and, specifically, public television, is more responsive to its environment than purposive—seeking optimal goals at minimal costs. Analysts should be less surprised by the policy trade-offs and accommodations that are required to sustain the existence of public television. Critics should recognize that public television officials cannot make strategic decisions that reflect strict adherence to an ideal form with unambiguous goals and optimal solutions. Public broadcasting bureaucrats primarily pursue policy goals that reflect the negotiated priorities and preferences of Congress, the executive, and the more influential special interest groups—the dominant coalition.

In public broadcasting, as in all public organizations, compromise and adaptation are essential strategic behaviors. Public television managers make the best of a less than perfect environment. These managers respond to the demands of coalition partners in proportion to public television's dependence upon the scarce resources they supply. The demands of Congress and the executive predominate because these coalition partners furnish indispensable monetary and linking resources. Managers of public television respond to the demands of particular special interest groups in accordance with their success in lobbying Congress and the executive. Moreover, Congress and the executive are only as actively involved in the strategic management of public broadcasting as the special interest groups demand by their pressure—given the host of other policy issues that compete for executive and congressional attention. The outcome of all the bargaining is that policies are only as coherent as the demands of the more persuasive special interest groups.

Public television has been more responsive to the dynamic demands of the dominant coalition members—Congress, the executive, and public television station managers—than to more marginal special interest groups. Organizations such as ACNO, the National Black Media Coalition, Latinos in Public Telecommunications, and some independent producer groups have exerted substantially less influence over the strategic behavior of public television than the regional networks of stations, production entities, and the Association of Public Broadcasting (formerly, NAPTS).

Because Congress statutorily dictates how public broadcasting must allocate critical federal funds, broadcasting officials have usually elected to bolster linkages with those special interest groups with greater congressional clout. Since the Nixon veto, the Corporation has progressively acquiesced to public television station dominance and coordinated most public television activities in collaboration with NAPTS. The Corporation also has worked closely with major production centers and production entities, whereas collaboration with minorities, women, and fledgling independent producers has waxed and waned with these groups' efforts in gaining Congress's attention and support.

For example, some filmmakers have benefitted from the uncertain funding of program production. The need to pool monies and engage in joint ventures to produce high-quality fare has transformed a few enterprising, well-established early entrants—public television stations and independent producers—into barons within the public television industry. Production entities, such as Public Television Playhouse (a joint venture that includes WGBH, WNET, and KCET), and independent producers, such as Bill Moyers, are applauded for their enterprise and business savvy by Corporation and PBS officials. In return for filling the void in public television programming, they are routinely awarded multimillion dollar production contracts.

Corporation funding to smaller independent producers, however, has not been sufficient to bring their projects from the production stage to broadcast. Lesser known filmmakers and some independents have asserted that Corporation funding is woefully inadequate. These producers also have claimed that they are left to fend for themselves—by begging and borrowing—in order to produce, distribute, and air their shows on public television.[2] Highly acclaimed producers, such as Stanley Karnow (the *Philippines* and *Vietnam* series), Henry Hampton (*Eyes on the Prize*), and Marlon Riggs (*Ethnic Notions*) have resorted to such methods. As Henry Hampton and Marlon Riggs have stated in congressional hearings, when they succeed in getting their productions aired on public television, they succeed in spite of the Corporation and PBS bureaucracies.[3]

THE ORGANIZATIONAL EFFECTIVENESS OF PUBLIC TELEVISION

Public television is an effective organization. Not only does this national system of public telecommunications survive, public television thrives. Despite budget uncertainty and political vulnerability, public television successfully discharges its legislative mandate. In fat budget years as well as leaner ones or politically favorable years as well as unfavorable ones, public television serves the public interest, convenience, and necessity. Hardly the inept entity threatened with impending demise frequently portrayed in print media headlines, public television is a well-managed collectivity of diverse interests that assumes whatever forms, missions, and means required for survival. Public television retains both its protected environment and support from coalition partners and, thereby, obtains increased federal funding.

Report Card on Public Television

The "report card" on public television reads: "A+" for survival, from the resource dependence perspective, and "C−" for strategic management, from the rational perspective. Public broadcasting policy makers, bureaucrats, and special interest groups are exceptionally good at maintaining a protected and financially secure environment for public television. Although public television does not always obtain the requested levels of federal funding, when compared with other public organizations by percentage increased annual appropriations, it does extraordinarily well. On strategic behavior, however, public television's record of performance on the attainment of employment, programming, and audience diversity goals is dubious.

Analysis of the Corporation for Public Broadcasting's appropriations history shows a highly successful public organization. Although much of the print media's rhetoric describes public broadcasting as significantly underfunded, this public organization has enjoyed atypical appropriations increases over time. From FY 1969 through FY 1989, the Corporation has averaged federal funding increases of 24 percent, whereas the mean for most public organizations hovers between 0 and 10 percent. When the Nixon veto and Reagan omnibus budget cuts are excluded, Corporation appropriations increases have averaged 40 percent for this period. Corporation appropriations have assumed an incremental trend only in recent years, primarily as an outcome of the fiscal conservatism introduced by the Reagan Administration.

In the twenty-five years since enactment of the 1967 Public Broadcasting Act, public television is a significantly enlarged, improved, and expanded system. Improvements in coverage extension, station interconnection, signal and programming quality, technical capacity, and audience penetration are but a few of its accomplishments. However, the persuasive proof of its organizational effectiveness is public television's growth. By 1989, public television had become a substantially larger and better financed system. Public television stations now number 341, more than a 500 percent increase over the number licensed in 1962 (56) and its federal budget is $228 million, a more than fortyfold increase over the 1969 appropriation of $5 million. In FY 1989, public television's total operating budget exceeded $236 million.

Examples of organizational effectiveness also are provided by public television officials' responsiveness to budgetary shortfalls. When allocations for program production have fallen short of the targeted amount, public broadcasting officials have added more foreign programming, commercial syndications, and reruns of prior PBS distributions to the schedule. When allocations to stations have failed to reach the necessary levels, station managers have found innovative ways to raise revenue: diversification into publishing ventures, for example, The Frugal Gourmet; commercial radio, for example, WTTW-TV ownership of WFMT-FM; "renting" activities, for example, leasing station production facilities to independent producers; acquiring and distributing programming and pooling program production are just a few examples of the more successful strategies.

When essential future federal financing becomes uncertain, managers of public television production entities also demonstrate their responsiveness to threatened changes in the public television environment. For example, one major station producer, WNET, continues to exploit revenue-generation opportunities. Whether solely to increase income or perhaps to offset potential shortfalls from Congress's line-item allocation to the Independent Production Service, WNET entered into a joint venture with Time Life Video in 1989. Together, they market video cassettes of old programs from the *Nature* series through their Nature Video Library.

Public Television is a Panacea and a Pork Barrel

Public television, in fact, is so effective that its successful track record as a public organization affords additional support for the conclusions drawn at the beginning of this chapter. Public television is a panacea and a pork barrel. Although these attributes may have negative connotations when applied to the private organization, they can have positive implications for the public organization. In the public organization, these attributes can also reflect the successful management of a dynamic, competitive, and uncertain environment.

As a policy and in practice, public television provides something for everyone and materially benefits special interest groups within the public broadcasting industry. By minimally satisfying some of the goals of all groups ("satisficing" behavior), public television maintains the coalition of support necessary for increased appropriations. Whether as direct benefits to the public, such as enhanced viewer choice and alternative programming, or direct subsidies to stations and production entities, public television offers something to all publics. Panacea and pork barrel also describe public television's record of compliance with the performance expectations of Congress and the executive. Although public television does not fully or consistently demonstrate the levels or types of compliance that all interested parties prefer, it routinely provides Congress and the executive with the minimal compliance these policy makers demand.

In short, the attributes panacea and pork barrel further attest to the organizational effectiveness of public television because they describe this public organization's responsiveness and adaptiveness. Whether confronted by political upheaval or budgetary retrenchment, public television makes the required adjustments. Public broadcasting managers continually identify alternative structures and means to ensure public television's survival. Although public broadcasting bureaucrats have made many of the adjustments unwillingly, under extreme duress, or with strident protest, nonetheless, public television has been overhauled and restructured to suit the tastes of policy makers and special interest groups.

The Negative Impact of Public Television's Search for Survival

In spite of the glowing successes, there remains room for improving the organizational effectiveness of public television. Weaknesses are also embedded in public television's panacea and pork barrel attributes. Two greatly debated outcomes have resulted from Corporation officials' sustained efforts to retain the coalition support from Congress, the executive, and influential special interest groups—especially, public television station executives—and to secure increased federal funding. They are the decentralization of public broadcasting organization and discretion and the deregulation of public television. Decentralization has contributed to the discretionary fragmentation of public television and losses in autonomy for the Corporation for Public Broadcasting. Deregulation has led to precarious practices of "underwriting" and "near advertising" by some public television stations, loosened restrictions on CSG expenditures, minimized enforcement of equal employment opportunity guidelines, and decreased domestically produced, innovative, and diverse programming.

Since inception, public television station executives have vied with Corporation officials for greater control over public broadcasting allocative and programming discretion. As the principal providers of public broadcasting services to consumers, station executives have sought to retain control over the expenditure of federal funds and broadcast of programming tailored to the unique tastes of local audiences. In open hearings on the House and Senate floors and in meetings behind closed doors with White House staff, public television managers have fought off efforts by public broadcasting officials to manage public television as a highly centralized, nationally controlled, and coordinated bureaucracy that dictates policy and programming tastes along normative lines—a "Fourth Network."

Public television station executives have enjoyed major victories in their battles with bureaucrats for control over public broadcasting policy. By consolidating their power as regional and national alliances and successfully lobbying Congress and the executive, station executives have progressively wrested budgetary and programming discretion from Corporation officials. The end product is a system that the Corporation itself describes as "the most decentralized, diversified broadcasting enterprise in the world."[4] Public television is not the centralized and well-coordinated "Fourth Network" envisioned by some early advocates. Instead, public television has evolved into a constellation of public broadcasting organizations created by the Corporation for Public Broadcasting and the stations that "literally belong to the stations."[5]

Over the years, the conflict between officials and public television special interest groups—center and periphery—has eroded the Corporation's authority and role in the definition and coordination of public broadcasting policy. As special interest groups have competed over goals, means, and benefits, the organizational, budgetary, and decision-making structures of the Corporation have been adjusted to accommodate the demands for reciprocity from the winners. Sensitive to demands from their constituents, Congress continues to parcel off Corporation internal management discretion and authority by earmarking funds for the more influential special interest groups. Even the more recent CPB appropriations legislation, PL 100–626, provides direct payments to public television stations and independent producers. Community service grants and program distribution (interconnection) funds are passed directly to the stations as fixed percentages of the Corporation's appropriations. Program production monies are now passed through to the independent and minority producers as fixed lump-sum payments. Thus, decentralization and discretionary fragmentation fuel the pork barrel allegations of media analysts.

Fragmented Discretion Under Deregulation: Value Trade-Offs. Since inception, decentralization and dispersed discretion and control in a climate of deregulation and fiscal conservatism have encouraged laissez faire and narrowly self-interested strategic behavior by public television station managers and other broadcasting professionals. In the absence of centralized coordination and widespread knowledge about public broadcasting organization, public broadcasting decision makers have not been held publicly accountable for their strategic behavior. The disbandment of ACNO further distanced the public from public television.

Although decentralization reflects organizational responsiveness, it also limits public television effectiveness. In addition to Corporation losses in internal management discretion, decentralization has diluted the diversity goals of public broadcasting by distributing decision making and control across an array of public television entities (discretionary fragmentation). Discretionary fragmentation diminishes Corporation oversight and station executives' accountability, and thereby constrains policy coordination and programming diversity.

In a deregulated environment characterized by enhanced station discretion and autonomy, public television station executives freely pursue whatever strategic behaviors they deem appropriate with minimal accountability, particularly to goals of employment, programming, and audience diversity. For example, congressional alterations of CPB management discretion have resulted in managerial and other cuts to CPB staff. Consequently, staff reductions have impaired CPB management efforts to oversee and enforce station compliance with expenditure and equal employment opportunity guidelines. As the data presented in Chapter 6 illustrate, it is not uncommon for a significant percentage of public television stations to employ no minority persons in managerial, technical, or even clerical positions. For many station executives, equal employment opportunity is defined as hiring more women.

As station managers gear programming to the tastes attributed to donor viewers, less programming is broadcast for children, minorities, seniors, and other audiences. As shown in Chapter 6, the percentage of programming broadcast for special audiences has declined substantially in recent years. Yet, adult informational and how-to programs have doubled. Fewer programs by, for, or about minorities are selected by station representatives for purchase by the SPC and those that are purchased have very limited carriage. A case in point is the series *South Africa Now*. In 1989, it was carried by only 30 of the 327 public television stations. Even in years when the Corporation provided matching funds (3:1) to stations that chose minority programming through the SPC, few station executives capitalized on the opportunity.

Station managers' reliance upon programming that is tried, true, and safe is so pervasive that public television is often described as hum drum, high brow, or lacking initiative and creativity. Station managers and producers routinely trade off creative, innovative, and diverse programming in favor of secure corporate funding. Producers of successful series, for example, *American Playhouse*, are more inclined toward "remakes" of previously celebrated works—*Death of a Salesman* and *Raisin in the Sun*—than production of new works by promising contemporary artists.

Further, some public television stations with limited program production capability and purchasing power are inclined toward the broadcast of higher percentages of risk-averse and cheap programming. Reruns of old movies, commercial syndications—for example, *Lawrence Welk, Leave it to Beaver, It's Showtime at the Apollo*, and the *Avengers*. BBC soap operas and other syndications are standard fare for some stations, particularly during lean years. Such programming does not make public television a viable alternative to commercial television; rather, it merely pads a wanting schedule and increases viewers' choice. As a supplement to commercial and cable television, viewers simply tune in for a particular show, then drop out or tune in while searching for a viewing alternative.[6]

In addition, deregulation coupled with diminished oversight has led to questionable "advertising" practices. During the Reagan Administration, public television station executives were charged to experiment with advertising and find other sources of revenue. The identification of sponsors, supporters, and underwriters as well as the use of logograms at the beginning and end of most public television shows are now commonplace. Occasional viewers are probably startled or perplexed when they see brand name products displayed on public television, such as a can of Pepsi Cola or a bottle of Durkee's hot sauce.[7] Public television stations have played so loosely with advertising restrictions—including the interruption of programming to announce the evening lineup, thank donors, or beg—that viewers find themselves looking at the dial to verify that they have tuned in to public television.

AN Rx FOR PUBLIC TELEVISION

How can the organizational effectiveness of public television be improved? Although some critics continue to recommend structural overhaul as "the remedy," public broadcasting has been restructured and reorganized to excess. Alternatively, public television can be greatly improved by enhancing strategic management and by providing better public accountability at all levels of organization: congressional, corporation, and station. Making greater efforts to achieve the diversity goals, expanding market share, disengaging station executives from the fundraising business, and the local production of more locally oriented programming are a few key modifications that would go far to improve public television and simultaneously make decision makers more publicly accountable for their strategic decisions.

Foremost, public broadcasting officials must acknowledge and recapture lost market share. Over the last decade, public television's market share has been encroached upon to the extent that its primary product, programming, is expendable. Notwithstanding the contributions made in the early days of educational television, there is very little programming now broadcast on public television that is unavailable from the commercial and cable television weekly lineups. This includes children's as well as adult cultural, informational, news and public affairs programming. *School Break Specials, Faerie Tale Theatre, Nova,* and *Nature;* drama, opera, BBC soaps, Shakespeare, and the American Ballet Theatre; financial and business programs; docudramas (the KAL disaster, Corizon Aquino's ascendancy in the Philippines, and Simon Wiesenthal); as well as in-depth news coverage and analyses, all are regularly available on cable and commercial television.

In short, public television decision makers need to acknowledge that considerable market share has been lost to cable and commercial broadcasting. Public television is no longer an exclusive vehicle for airing fare that commercial broadcasters deem unprofitable. Nor is it the vehicle that broadcasts programming that is not available elsewhere. When public television executives must make substantial commitments to fundraising activities, other activities and resources critical to sustaining and increasing market share are sacrificed. Resources are not allocated to the continuance of educational television's legacy of trail-blazing programming, but toward the production and broadcast of "safely splendid" fare.

To improve public television, station executives need to get out of the fund-raising business and do a better job of promoting and encouraging localism, that is, localism defined as including the diversity of the "publics" served by the coverage areas and not exclusively defined as either the discretion and autonomy of public television station licensees and managers or viewer checkwriters. Station executives could increase their market share by broadcasting higher percentages of diverse programming and, thereby, broadening the audience demographics. Just like its commercial and cable competitors, public television requires constant infusions of new and innovative programs. As *DeGrassi Junior High, 21 Jump Street, The Cosby Show, Different World*, and *Rosanne* have illustrated, programming diversity increases audience share. Interestingly, the programming categories that could earn public television more market share are the very ones whose percentage broadcast hours have declined during the last decade: the unserved and underserved audiences of children, seniors, and minority groups.

In recent years, "localism" in public television is more myth than reality. By pandering programming to a "national profile" shaped by donor viewers and corporate underwriters, "localism" in programming—defined as "public" participation—is sorely lacking. Of the programming broadcast on public television, the most highly and critically acclaimed programming is produced for the "national" audience of donor viewers. Major public television producers, production entities, and independent producers all shoot for the largest possible national audience. Only a small percentage of programming broadcast on public television is produced by, for, or about the local audiences served by "community" stations. Moreover, public television stations might try providing some form of innovative, high-quality, nonmerchandising "public-access" programming, for example, forums on local issues, showcasing local artists, and other topics unique to the coverage area.

Again, the pioneering programs produced and aired in the early days of educational television were also more responsive to local communities. Although much of this programming was "low-quality" given the paltry budgets and technical limitations of the early educational television stations, these stations featured more station-produced programs on local artists, events, and issues. As long as public television station managers continue to cater programming to the tastes of donor viewers and the interests of corporate underwriters, local audiences will remain underserved by public television.

Indeed, if public television is to provide a truly "local" service, then the stations should be held more accountable to their local audience. This, too, is a strategic management issue, not a structural problem. In many communities, the public is ill-informed about board meetings despite the legal requirement to announce them. Station executives should actively promote more public participation by making board meetings more visible and board membership more representative of the communities they serve. Although a substantial number of public television community stations have multicultural or significant minority populations, many boards of directors have few minority or female members.

In order to achieve the diversity in programming, employment, and audience goals, the management of public television stations and its boards must become more culturally inclusive and truly reflect the demographics of the coverage areas. As demonstrated earlier, historically, public television has failed to achieve programming, employment, or audience diversity. Corporation officials, congressional leaders, and members of special interest groups have criticized station executives for their poor records on minority programming and employment.

As in commercial broadcasting, public television's managerial hierarchy lacks sufficient minority input and, thereby, constrains organizational effectiveness. The "bland homogeneity" and "elitism" that are said to characterize public television programming are attributable, in part, to established employment patterns within public broadcasting management. As the prior analyses of public television employment statistics have also shown, minority persons hold fewer than 5 percent of the stations' managerial positions nationwide. African, Asian, Hispanic, Native American, and other ethnic minorities have played very minor roles in public television station management discretion. Because general, operations, and programming managers make decisions based on their experiences, values, beliefs, and knowledge, the managerial hierarchy must become more heterogeneous before public television can accomplish its mission.

Furthermore, Congress must demand and the Corporation for Public Broadcasting must provide and coordinate greater oversight. As the legal guardians of the public coffers and airwaves, Congress has the job of requiring that the public organization be in compliance and accountable to its legal mandate. Periodic managerial alterations and occasional tinkering with Corporation internal management detail, in response to pressure from special interest groups, is not sufficient oversight. As demonstrated by the Social Security Administration's "policy of silence on SSI benefits for the homeless" as well as recent HUD and thrifts (savings and loans) scandals, Congress must do a better job of scrutinizing the strategic behavior of bureaucrats, managers, and agents.

Playing Robin Hood with CPB internal management discretion only weakens the Corporation's ability to manage the systems. When it is public television station executives who are accused of using federal monies to refurbish offices and hire limousines at the taxpayers' expense, why are Corporation administrative guidelines tightened and station CSG expenditure restrictions loosened? Why are side payments to special interest groups subtracted from the Corporation's management capacity? Why reallocate line items from CPB management to special interest groups, thereby eliminating the very staff and managerial roles charged to monitor and ensure public television station compliance with public broadcasting policy? Such congressional strategic behavior merely robs Peter to pay Paul. Not only do special interest redistributive decisions ignore important contextually dependent valuations—who is rich and who is poor—they also ignore important potential outcomes—who benefits at what costs.

Because public television is a hodgepodge of dispersed public broadcasting activity, the public has low, or certainly limited, expectations for performance. Not only is the public ill-informed about what public television does, it is uninformed about what it is supposed to do. Given public broadcasting's broad and obscure goals—service in the public interest, convenience, and necessity—public standards for public television performance are minimal, if extant at all. Although public television is not legally established as a public trust, Corporation managers are still entrusted with the responsibility to provide diverse and innovative, cultural, educational, and informational programming to diverse audiences—not a monolithic audience.

CONCLUSION

Public television performance is greatly constrained by managers' need to dance to the myriad tunes played by Congress, the executive, and special interest groups—resource dependence. More than any other goal, managers of public television entities pursue organizational survival. Public television's mandate to provide programming, employment, and audience diversity is subordinate to securing increased appropriations from one year to the next.

Public television managers' capitulations to changes in policy preferences caused by executive and legislative turnover have resulted in programming that is tried and true as well as bland and elitist. Local station managers most dependent upon federal—and to a lesser extent, state—dollars for their basic operation take fewer programming risks. In order to adjust to budget crises induced by executive and legislative tinkering in the management details of public broadcasting, station managers and producers routinely trade off creative, innovative, and diverse programming in favor of secure federal, corporate, and subscription funding. When mired in budget crises or controversy, managers broadcast syndicated reruns, old movies, and foreign productions to offset shortfalls or avoid controversy by selecting "safe" programming. In order to play it safe, station managers gear more programming to "upscale" donor viewers (subscribers) than to children, minorities and seniors—unserved and underserved audiences.

Once public broadcasting managers have complied with congressional and executive policy expectations, however, these decision makers then pursue whatever additional goals and strategies they choose, and distribute the benefits accordingly. Consequently, the stations, public television-related entities, and professionals within the industry receive substantial material benefits from public television, small independent producers and minorities in broadcasting receive more marginal benefits, and viewer checkwriters get a few more nature and culture shows added to the programming menu.

In conclusion, the strategic management of public television by decision makers who primarily pursue survival goals is not sufficient. As illustrated, the attainment of survival goals does not also guarantee the attainment of the goals specified in the legislative mandate. Public broadcasting decision makers at all levels of organization must be held more accountable to the public. Managers must recognize that special interest or constituency politics can be pursued in tandem with rationality norms. Bureaucrats and agents of public organizations are public caretakers and servants, not managers narrowly concerned about the bottom line. Like their private counterparts, decision makers in public organizations are concerned about profitability and the efficient use of insufficient federal dollars. Yet, reelection, job retention, material benefits, and aspirations for control over both policy means and ends hold too much sway over decision making in public organizations. Such self-interests should not be the predominant determinants of performance in public organizations.

Although special interests and issues are in competition for congressional attention and largess, policy makers should exercise greater adherence to social as well as economic—not primarily political—criteria in their evaluations of targets, costs, and benefits. Policy makers should identify, prioritize, and pursue goals and strategies that make the American public substantially better off by subordinating the bargaining requisites of special interests politics to moderately rational determinations of public well-being—the "common good" in accordance with norms that are defined as "satisfactory" not "best" (optimal). Foremost, policy makers must negotiate policy goals and means that retain public accountability, in the absence of subservience to more narrow special interests, in order to make public organizations more effective instruments of public policy.

NOTES

1. A public trust is constituted for the benefit of either the public at large or some considerable portion of it. A trust is a right of property, real or personal, held by one party for the benefit of another. It is any arrangement whereby

property is transferred with the intention that it be administered by trustee for another's benefit.

2. It is important to note that independent producers who are new to the CPB production funding apparatus have high expectations of the actual sums available. Unsolicited grants are a much smaller pool of funds, in which grants range, on average, from a few thousand to $150,000. However, the Corporation solicits programming from established producers, generally as multiyear contracts for significantly larger sums. On average, solicited grants range from $1 million to $2.5 million.

3. See *Current*, December 8, 1987, p. 13, and Senate Hearings, March 15, 1987.

4. See Corporation for Public Broadcasting, 1989.

5. Ibid.

6. This behavior is captured by the audience statistic, household cume. This statistic was expressly developed to measure public television viewing patterns because public television viewers watch significantly less television than viewers of commercial television. Cume measures the percentage viewing households that watch public television for six or more minutes per viewing session.

7. The Durkee's company is a sponsor for the how-to-cook show, *Justin Wilson*.

APPENDIX: CARNEGIE RECOMMENDATIONS

The Carnegie Commission, entrusted with the task of operationalizing the FCC Acts of 1927, 1934, 1951, and Comsat recommended in their 1967 report on educational television:

1. Concerted efforts at the federal, state, and local levels to improve the facilities and provide for adequate support of the individual educational television stations and to increase their number.

2. Congress to authorize and establish a federally chartered, nonprofit, nongovernmental corporation, to be known as the "Corporation for Public Television." The Corporation would be empowered to receive and disburse governmental and private funds.

3. That the Corporation support at least two national production centers, and that it be free to contract with independent producers to prepare public television programs.

4. That the Corporation support, by appropriate grants and contracts, the production of public television programs by local stations for more-than-local use.

5. The Corporation on appropriate occasions to help support local programming by local stations.

6. The Corporation to provide the educational television system as expeditiously as possible with facilities for live interconnection by conventional means, and that it be enabled to benefit from advances in technology as domestic communications satellites are brought into being.

7. The Corporation to encourage and support research and development leading to the improvement of programming and production.

8. The Corporation to support technical experimentation designed to improve the present television technology.

9. The Corporation to undertake to provide means by which technical, artistic, and specialized personnel may be recruited and trained.

10. Congress to provide the federal funds required by the Corporation through a manufacturers' excise tax on television sets (beginning at 2 percent and rising to a ceiling of 5 percent). The revenue should be made available to the Corporation through a trust fund.

11. New legislation to enable the Department of Health, Education, and Welfare to provide adequate facilities for stations now in existence; to assist in increasing the number of stations to achieve nationwide coverage; to help support the basic operations of all stations; and to enlarge the support of instructional television programming.

12. Federal, state, local, and private educational agencies sponsor extensive and innovative studies intended to develop better insight into the use of television in formal and informal education.

The Carnegie Commission also suggested a modified pyramidal hierarchical structure for decision-making and roles as shown in Figure A.1.

Figure A.1
The Corporation for Public Television

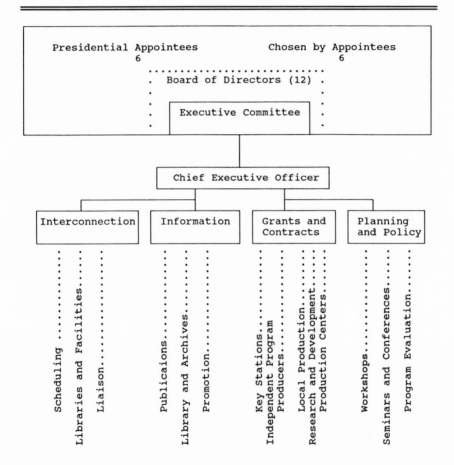

References

Aldrich, Howard, 1979, *Organizations and Environments* (Englewood Cliffs, NJ: Prentice-Hall).

Aharoni, Yair, 1971, *The Israeli Manager* (Tel Aviv: Israeli Institute of Business Research, Tel Aviv University).

Barnouw, Eric, 1966, *A Tower in Babel* (New York: Oxford University Press).

Blau, Peter M., 1968, "The Hierarchy of Authority in Organizations," *American Journal of Sociology*, 73 (January): 453–467.

———, 1970, "A Formal Theory of Differentiation in Organizations," *American Sociological Review*, 35 (April): 201–218.

Blakely, Robert J., 1979, *To Serve the Public Interest: Educational Broadcasting in the United States* (Syracuse, NY: Syracuse University Press).

Bozeman, Barry, 1987, *All Organizations are Public* (San Francisco: Jossey-Bass).

Broadcasting, 1971, May 24, pp. 42–43; 1972, July 3, p. 6; July 10, p. 35; July 31, p. 39; 1973, January 29, p. 60; April 23, pp. 21–22; May 21, pp. 36–37; June 4, p. 45; August 6, p. 21; August 13, pp. 23–24; 1987, November 16, p. 23.

Carnegie Commission on Educational Television, 1967, *Public Television: A Program for Action* (New York: Bantam).

Carnegie Commission Report, 1979, *A Public Trust* (New York: Bantam).

Carson, Emmett, 1989, "Black Philanthropy: Shaping Tomorrow's Nonprofit Sector," *Journal of Contemporary Issues in Fund Raising* (Summer): 23–31.

Cater, Douglas, and Nyhan, Michael, 1976, *The Future of Public Broadcasting* (New York: Praeger).

Chubb, John, and Moe, Terry, 1986. "Politics, Markets, and the Organization of Schools," *Brookings Discussion Papers in Governmental Studies* (Washington, D.C.: Brookings Institution).

Chubb, John, and Peterson, Paul (eds.), 1985, *The Directions in American Politics* (Washington, D.C.: Brookings Institution).

Coase, Ronald H., 1959, "The Federal Communications Commission," *Journal of Law and Economics*, 2(10): 1–41.

Cohen, Michael, and March, James, 1974, *Leadership and Ambiguity* (New York: McGraw-Hill).

Cohen, Michael D., March, James G., and Olsen, Johan P., 1972, "A Garbage Can Model of Organizations," *Administrative Science Quarterly* (March): 1–25.

——, 1979, *Ambiguity and Choice in Organizations* (Oslo, Norway: Universitetsforlaget).

Congressional Hearings Documents: Second Supplemental Appropriations Bill, 1972–1973, 1976, and 1981; Office of Education, Special Institutions and Related Agencies Appropriations, 1972, 1973, 1975, 1981, 1984, and 1987 (Washington, D.C.: U.S. Government Printing Office).

Congressional Record, *Legislative History, Corporation for Public Broadcasting*, 1967–1987 (Washington D.C.: U.S. Government Printing Office).

Corporation for Public Broadcasting, 1975, *Public Broadcasting and Education* (Washington, D.C.: CPB).

——, 1976–1986, *PTV Financial Summary* (Washington, D.C.: CPB).

——, 1980–1988, *Program Fund News* (Washington, D.C.: CPB).

——, 1987, *CPB Report* (Washington, D.C.: CPB).

——, 1988, *Audience 88, A Comprehensive Analysis of Public Radio Listeners* (Washington, D.C.: CPB).

——, 1989, *An Introduction to Public Broadcasting* (Washington, D.C.: CPB).

Corporation for Public Broadcasting Board, 1985, *By-Laws*.

Current, 1987, "What They Said on Capitol Hill," December 8: 7–22.

Cyert, Richard M., and March, James A., 1963, *A Behavioral Theory of the Firm* (Englewood Cliffs, NJ: Prentice-Hall).

Dorfmann, Ron, 1973, "Gelding Public TV," *Chicago Journalism Review* (April): 3–5.

Downs, Anthony, 1967, *Inside Bureaucracy* (Boston: Little Brown).

Dunagan, Craig, 1983, "Commercialization of Public Broadcasting," *Comment*, 5(2): 241–291.

Durkheim, Emile, 1949 (first published 1893), *Division of Labor in Society* (Glencoe, IL: Free Press).

Emerson, Richard. M., 1962, "Power Dependence Relations," *American Sociological Review*, 27: 31–41.

Esplin, Fred C., 1975, "Long Range Funding: The Forgotten Chapter," *Public Telecommunications Review*, 3(4): 22–27.

Federal Communications Commission, 1946, *Public Service Responsibility of Broadcast Licensees* (Washington, D.C.: U.S. Government Printing Office).

Federal Register, 1967–1986, *Weekly Compilation of Presidential Documents* (Washington, D.C.: Federal Register).

Fisher, Gregory, and Kamlet, Mark, 1982, *Explaining Presidential Priorities: Competing Aspiration Level Model of Macro-Budgetary Decision Making*, unpublished manuscript.

Ford Foundation, 1976, *Ford Foundation Activities in Noncommercial Broadcasting, 1951–1976* (New York: Ford Foundation).

Frank, Ronald, and Greenberg, Marshall, 1982, *Audiences for Public Television* (Beverly Hills: Sage).

Gans, Herbert, 1974, *Popular Culture and High Culture* (New York: Basic Books).

Gibson, George H., 1975, *Public Broadcasting* (New York: Praeger).

Goggin, Malcolm, 1987, *Policy Implementation by Design* (Knoxville: University of Tennessee Press).

Gouldner, Alvin, 1959, "Organizational Analysis," in *Sociology Today*, Robert K. Merton, Leonard Broom, and Leonard Cottrell, Jr. (Eds.) (New York: Basic Books), pp. 400–428.

Gortner, Harold, Mahler, Julianne, and Nicholson, Jeanne, 1987, *Organization Theory: A Public Perspective* (Chicago: Dorsey Press).

Grusky, Oscar, and Miller, George, 1977, *The Sociology of Organizations* (New York: Academic Press).

Guimary, Donald, 1975, *Citizens' Groups and Broadcasting* (New York: Praeger).

Gunn, Hartford, 1974, "Inside the Station Program Cooperative: An Interview with Hartford Gunn," *Public Telecommunications Review* (August): 16–24.

Hall, Richard, 1977, *Organizations: Structure and Process* (Englewood Cliffs, NJ: Prentice-Hall).

Heclo, Hugh, 1977, *A Government of Strangers: Executive Politics in Washington* (Washington D.C.: Brookings Institution).

Hirsch, Paul, 1980, "An Organizational Perspective on Television," in *Television and Social Behavior*, Stephen Withey and Ronald Abels (Eds.) (Hillsdale, NJ: Lawrence Erlbaum Associates), pp. 83–102.

——, 1975, "Organizational Effectiveness and the Institutional Environment," *Administrative Science Quarterly*, 20: 327–344.

Hirshman, Albert, 1970, *Exit, Voice, and Loyalty* (Cambridge, MA: Harvard University Press).

Hitt, Jack, 1987, "And Now, for Something Completely Cheap," *Harpers Magazine* (November): 58–59.

Jacobs, David, 1974, "Dependency and Vulnerability: An Exchange Approach to the Control of Organizations," *Administrative Science Quarterly*, 19 (March): 45–59.

Katz, Daniel, and Kahn, Robert, 1878, *The Social Psychology of Organizations* (New York: Wiley).

Katzman, Nathan, and Katzman, Solomon, 1974–1986, *Public Television Programming Content by Category* (Washington, D.C.: Corporation for Public Broadcasting).

Kaufman, Herbert, 1976, *Are Government Organizations Immortal?* (Washington, D.C.: Brookings Institution).

Key, V. O, 1964, *Politics, Parties, and Pressure Groups* (New York: Crowell).

Kritz, Margaret E., 1988, "Sparring Among Public Broadcasters," *National Journal*, 13 (August): 2100.

Lashley, Marilyn, 1986, *Predilection for Predictability: An Analysis of Decision-Making in Government-Financed Organizations*, unpublished dissertation, the University of Chicago.

LeLoupe, Lance, and Moreland, William, 1978, "Agencies, Strategies, and Executive Review: The Hidden Politics of Budgeting," *Public Administration Review*, 37: 232–239.

Lewin, Kurt, 1948, *Resolving Social Conflicts* (New York: Harper).

Lindblom, Charles, 1959, "The Science of Muddling Through," *Public Administration Review*, 19(2): 79–88.

————, 1968 *The Policy Making Process* (Englewood Cliffs, NJ: Prentice-Hall).

Lorch, Robert S., 1978, *Public Administration* (St. Paul, MN: West Publishing).

Lowi, Theodore, 1964, "American Business, Public Policy, Case Studies, and Political Theory," *World Politics*, 16 (July): 677–715.

Macy, John, 1974, *To Irrigate a Wasteland* (Berkeley: University of California Press).

March, James G., 1965, *Handbook of Organizations* (Chicago: Rand McNally).

March, James G., and Olsen, Johan P., 1976. *Ambiguity and Choice in Organizations* (Oslo, Norway: Universitetsforlaget).

March, James G., and Simon, Herbert, 1958, *Organizations* (New York: Wiley).

Marquis, Charlmers, 1979, *Brief History of Public Broadcasting Federal Financing Legislation, 1958–78* (Washington, D.C.: National Association of Public Television Stations).

Michels, Robert, 1962, *Political Parties* (New York: The Free Press).

Natchez, Peter, and Bupp, Irwin, 1973, "Policy and Priority in the Budgetary Process," *American Political Science Review*, 67: 951–963.

Network Project, 1971, *The Fourth Network* (New York: Columbia University Network Project, N.Y.C.).

Noll, Roger, Peck, Merton, and McGowan, John, 1973, *Economic Aspects of Television Regulation* (Washington, D.C.: Brookings Institution).

Padgett, John, 1981, "Hierarchy and Ecological Control in Federal Budgetary Decision-Making," *American Journal of Sociology*, 87: 75–189.

Pareto, Vilfredo, 1971, *Manual of Political Economy*, A. Schwier and A. Page (Eds.) (New York: A. M. Kelley).

Parsons, Talcott, 1956, "Suggestions for a Sociological Approach to the Theory of Organizations," *Administrative Science Quarterly*, 1 (June): 63–85.

Pepper, Robert, 1983, *The Formation of Public Broadcasting* (New York: Arno Press).

Perrow, Charles, 1970, *Organizational Analysis: A Sociological View* (Belmont, CA: Wadsworth).

Pfeffer, Jeffery, 1972, "Interorganizational Influence and Managerial Attitudes," *Academy of Management Journal*, 15: 317–330.

————, 1972, "Merger as a Response to Organizational Interdependence," *Administrative Science Quarterly*, 17 (September): 382–392.

Pfeffer, Jeffery, and Salancik, Gerald, 1978, *The External Contol of Organizations* (New York: Harper & Row).

Public Broadcasting Service, 1985–1987, *SPC Program Catalog*, Numbers 13, 14, and 15.

————, 1987, *A Study of Member Viewing Habits*, November.

————, 1988, *National Audience Report* April 18–24; June 7–24.

————, 1988, *Program Producers Handbook*, January.

Rainey, Hal G., Backoff, Robert W., and Levine, Charles H., 1976, "Comparing Public and Private Organizations," *Public Administration Review*, 36: 233–244.

Randall, R., 1973, "Influence of Environmental Support and Policy Space on Organizational Behavior," *Administrative Science Quarterly*, 18: 236–247.

Ripley, Randall, and Franklin, Grace, 1975, *Policy Making in the Federal Executive Branch* (New York: The Free Press).

Rowland, Willard, 1976, in Douglas Cater and Michael Nyan (eds.) *The Future of Public Broadcasting* (New York: Praeger).

———, 1975, "Public Involvement: The Anatomy of a Myth," *Public Telecommunications Review* (May/June): 6–21.

Sadowsky, Shelly, 1983, *Public Broadcasting's Battle Against Recision—1981*, unpublished manuscript, University of Maryland, School of Law.

Salancik, Gerald, 1976, "The Role of Interdependencies in Organizational Responsiveness to Demands from Environment: The Case of Women Versus Power," unpublished manuscript, University of Illinois.

Salancik, Gerald, and Lamont, Valerie, 1975, "Conflicts in Societal Research," *Journal of Higher Education*, 46(2): 161–176.

Samuelson, Robert, 1989, "Highbrow Pork Barrel," *Washington Post*, August 16: A9.

Schattschneider, E. E., 1960, *The Semi-Sovereign People* (New York: Holt, Rinehart, & Winston).

Schick, Allen, 1985, *Crisis in the Budget Process* (Washington, D.C.: American Enterprise Institute).

Schramm, Wilbur, and Nelson, Lyle, 1972, *The Financing of PTV* (Palo Alto, CA: Stanford University Press).

Schull, Steven, 1978, "Presidential–Congressional Support for Agencies and for Each Other: A Comparative Look," *Journal of Politics*, 40: 753–760.

Scott, Chris, 1989, "Listeners File Suit Against WFMT's Owner," *Crains Chicago Business*, June 29: 61.

Scott, W. Richard, 1981, *Organizations, Rational, Natural, and Open Systems* (Englewood Cliffs, NJ: Prentice-Hall).

Seidmann, Harold, 1988, "Neither Fish Nor Fowl," *The Brookings Review* (Summer): 6–9.

Selznick, Phillip, 1949, *TVA and the Grass Roots* (Berkeley: University of California Press).

Simon, Herbert, 1964, "On the Concept of Organizational Goal," *Administrative Science Quarterly*, 9: 1–22.

Smith, Anthony, 1973, *The Shadow in the Cave* (Urbana: University of Illinois Press).

Taylor, Fredrick, 1911, *Principles of Scientific Management* (New York: Harper Row).

Thompson, James D., 1967, *Organizations in Action* (New York: McGraw-Hill).

U. S. Congress. House, Subcommittee of the Committee on Appropriations, *Departments of Labor, Health and Human Services, Education and Related Agencies, Appropriations*, Hearings on Public Broadcasting, 1967–1988 (Washington, D.C.: U.S. Government Printing Office).

U.S. Congress. House, Subcommittee Telecommunications, Committee on Energy and Commerce, 1967–1988 (Washington, D.C.: U.S. Government Printing Office).

U. S. Congress. Senate, Reports, Committee on Commerce, Science, and Transportation, *Departments of Labor, Health and Human Services, Education and Related Agencies Appropriations Bills*, FY67–88 (Washington, D.C.: U.S. Government Printing Office).

U.S. Congress. Senate, Subcommittee on Communications of the Committee on

Commerce, Science, and Transportation, *Hearings on Public Broadcasting*, 1967–1988, (Washington D.C.: U.S. Government Printing Office).

U.S. Congress. Senate, Subcommittee on Communications of the Committee on Commerce, Science, and Transportation, *Hearings, Advertising and Public Broadcasting*, 1984 (Washington D.C.: U.S. Government Printing Office).

U.S. Statutes. *Public Broadcasting Act*, 90–129, 91–437, 92–411, 93–84, 94–192, 95–567, 97–35, 98–214, 99–272, and 100–626 (Washington, D.C.: U.S. Government Printing Office).

Video Networks, 1987 (June/July): 21–25.

von Bertalanffy, Ludwig, 1950, "The Theory Open Systems in Physics and Biology," *Science* 111: 23–28.

———, 1956, "General System Theory. General Systems," *Yearbook of the Society for General Systems Theory*, 1: 1–10.

The Washington Lobby, 4th ed. Congressional Quarterly, Inc.

Weber, Max, 1947 (first published in 1924), *The Theory of Social and Economic Organization*, A. H. Henderson and Talcott Parsons (Eds.) (Glencoe, IL: The Free Press).

Weingast, Barry R., Shepsle, Kenneth A., and Johnen, Christopher, 1981, "The Political Economy of Benefits and Costs: A Neoclassical Approach to Distributive Politics," *Journal of Political Economy*, 89(41): 642–664.

Weisman, John, 1987, "A Four-Month Survey Reveals a Failure to Cope with Serious Problems," *TV Guide* (August 1): 2–11, and (August 8): 26–40.

Wildavsky, Aaron, 1974, *Politics of the Budgetary Process* (Boston: Little Brown).

———, 1975, *Budgeting: A Comparative Theory of the Budgetary Process* (Boston: Little Brown).

White, Joseph, 1988, "What Budgeting Cannot Do: Lessons of Reagan's and Other Years," in *New Directions in Budget Theory*, Irene S. Rubin (Ed.) (Ithaca: State University of New York Press), pp. 165–202.

White, Stephen, 1977, "Carnegie II: A Look Back and Ahead," *Public Telecommunications Review* (August): 6–10.

———, 1987, "Our Public Television Experiment," *Public Interest*, 88: 79–93.

Witherspoon, John, and Kovitz, Roselle, 1989, *The History of Public Broadcasting* (Washington, D.C.: Current).

Zald, Mayer, and Wamsley, Gary, 1973, *The Political Economy of Public Organizations* (Lexington, MA: Lexington).

Index

ABOUT THE AUTHOR

MARILYN LASHLEY is an Assistant Professor in the Public Policy concentration of the Afro-American Studies Program at the University of Maryland, College Park. She specializes in research on a number of major public policy questions.